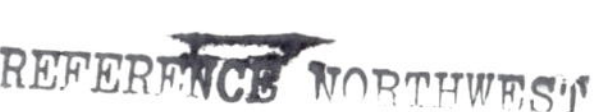

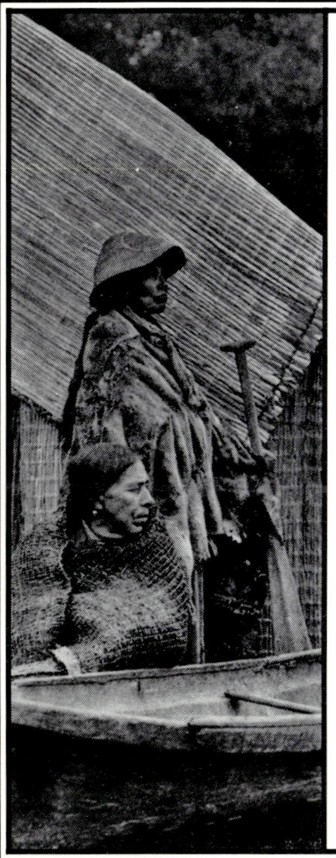

LOST PERSPECTIVES

The Art and Culture of Western Washington Indians

Presented by the

Washington State Historical Society

315 North Stadium Way

Tacoma, Washington

Exhibit Dates: June 17 to August 30, 1986

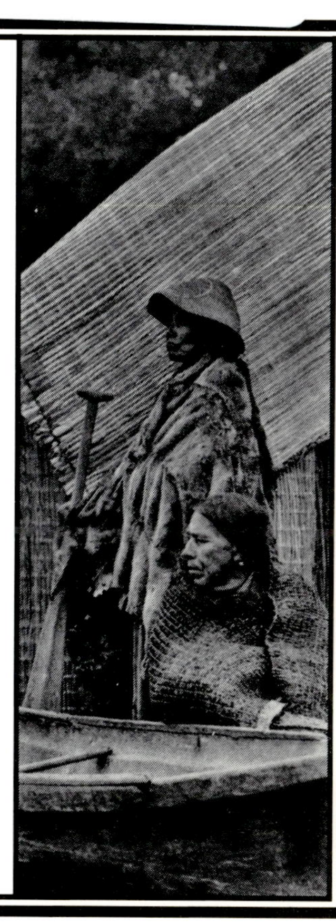

Catalog Text: Nile Thompson

Captions: Darrel Thiel

Design: R. Frederick

ISBN # 0-917048-60-1

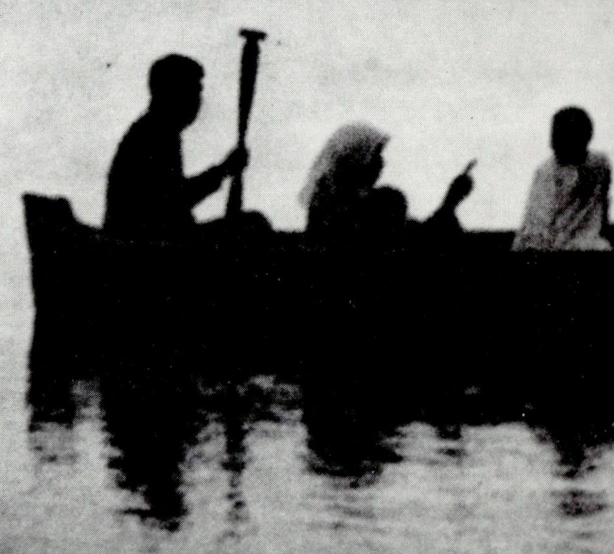

Photo: Sunset on Puget Sound. Edward Curtis.
Cover: On the Skokomish River. Edward Curtis.

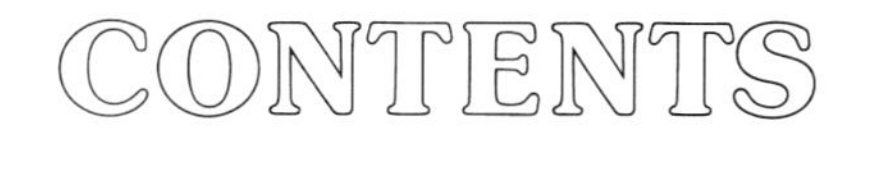
CONTENTS

ACKNOWLEDGMENTS

In early 1985, our Society's Curator of Collections, Darrel Thiel, recommended that we embark on a project which would display the clothing, tools, and religious pieces that are illustrative of the Indian culture of Western Washington. His impetus to suggest such an endeavor arose from the fact that recent exhibitions on Northwest Native Cultures have concentrated primarily on the tribes of the British Columbian and Alaskan coasts. This may have given the public the impression that there is little of significance left to us by Western Washington's tribes.

Through Darrel's efforts and through the cooperation and support of the many museums and private collections represented in our exhibit, LOST PERSPECTIVES: THE ART AND CULTURE OF WESTERN WASHINGTON INDIANS, we are able to celebrate the achievements of a people that have long been overlooked by scholars and the public.

In presenting this exhibit, the Society is proud to take a leading role in the dissemination of knowledge aimed at better understanding the people who lived in our region prior to white settlement, and whose descendants still live among us, and continue to contribute to our rich cultural landscape.

The Society is ever grateful to Darrel for his work in this area and to its Curator of Photography, Richard Frederick, whose photographs have helped to illustrate the exhibition and this catalog.

Equally important are the institutions and collectors who have played a critical role in making this exhibit possible. They are the Cowlitz County Historical Society in Kelso, Eastern Washington State Historical Society in Spokane, Makah Cultural Center in Neah Bay, the Thomas Burke Memorial Washington State Museum at the University of Washington in Seattle, the Washington State Capital Museum in Olympia, Jack Curtright, Natalie Linn, Mel Marquis, Delbert J. McBride, Lee Miner, and Jerrie and Anne Vander Houwen.

Finally, none of this could be possible without the generous support we have received from Pacific First Federal Bank, the Washington State Arts Commission, the Greater Tacoma Community Foundation, and the Tacoma Arts Commission.

Tony King
Director
Washington State
Historical Society

FOREWORD

This catalog accompanies an exhibit sponsored by the Washington State Historical Society. To make this exhibit possible, the society used not only objects from its own collection but brought in many items from other museums and from private collections throughout the state.

Lost Perspectives was organized as direct result of recent exhibitions such as "Willie Seaweed," "Objects of Great Pride" and "The Box of Daylight." These exhibits brought out the fact that a great deal of research has been done on the Indians of Canada and Alaska, but virtually nothing has been done regarding the tribes of Western Washington. Lost Perspectives is the first exhibit, by a museum in the Pacific Northwest, to highlight the grandeur and variety of implements, baskets, clothing, and spiritual items which were created by the Indian people of Western Washington during the last century.

While many of the artifactual pieces can be enjoyed as art pieces in themselves, it is the purpose of this exhibit that the objects will also be appreciated because of their traditional use within the culture.

Darrel Thiel
Curator of Collections
Washington State
Historical Society

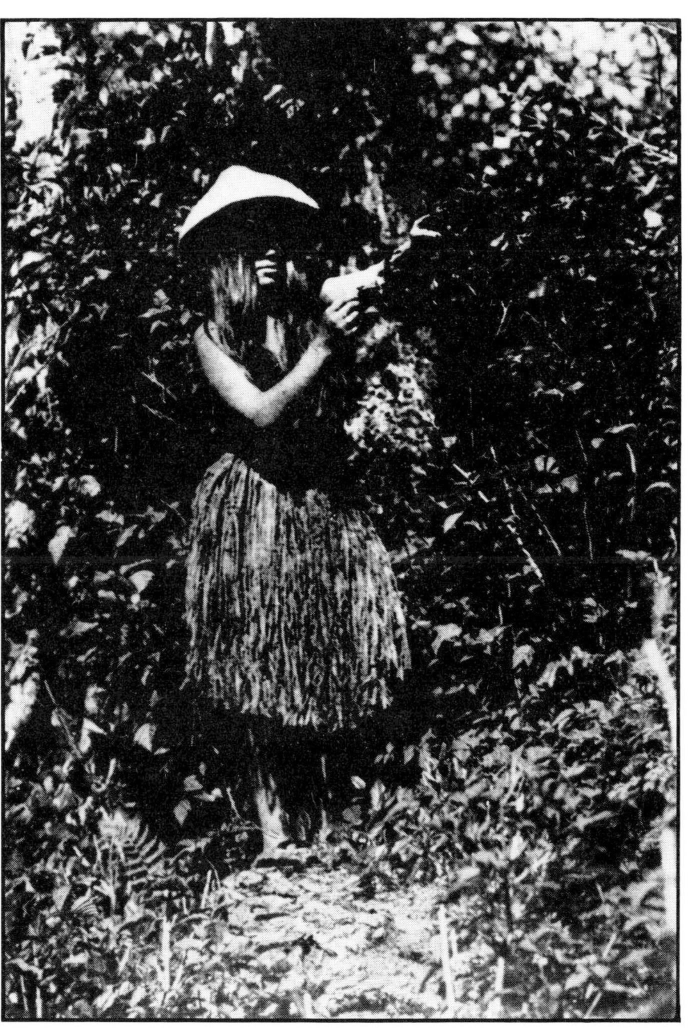

Quinault Berry Picker. Edward Curtis.

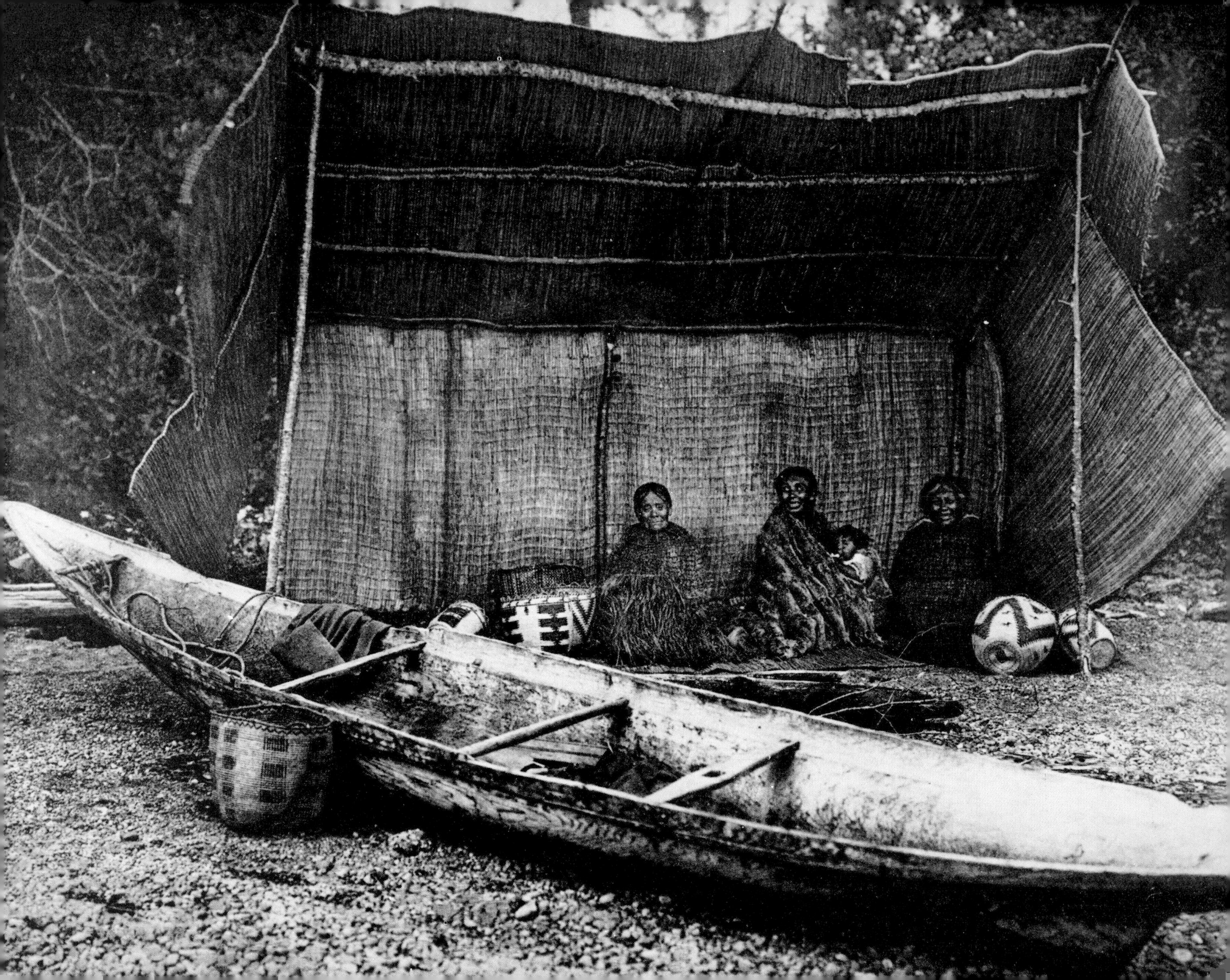

LOST PERSPECTIVES

Many of the individuals who find an ancient object of Native American manufacture in its natural habitat readily make an association between the object and its traditional use. Who made it? How was it used? How was it made? How did it come to be here? The same object observed in a museum, however, may evoke quite a different response. It is often judged for aesthetic appreciation alone or viewed in contrast to similar modern items made by non-Indians.

"Lost Perspectives" is an exhibit that deals with objects of utility and ceremony made by the Native Americans of western Washington State. It seeks to reestablish the tie between many types of objects and their place in the traditional culture.

With this exhibit, the Washington State Historical Society provides a view of relics from peoples whose art, ceremony and technology have received little attention when compared to their coastal neighbors to the distant north, namely the Kwagutl, Haida, Tsimshian and Tlingit. The failure of local museums to systematically collect and exhibit artifacts from western Washington prompted one anthropologist earlier this century to write:

> [S]urprisingly . . . the institutions within the State of Washington . . . have a considerable array of material objects from various possible and impossible places, but they exhibit little from their own vicinity. Apparently [none] has ever carried on intelligent collecting in its own neighborhood.

To remedy past errors by supplementing its own collection, the Washington State Historical Society has gathered a number of objects from other museums and private collections from throughout the state.

Utilitarian pieces without any elaboration have sometimes been labeled "crudely made." For this reason, many ancient utilitarian objects failed to attract the attention of collectors and have disappeared altogether. Even individuals who have worked in Indian communities, and have read descriptions of certain archaic items, may not fully comprehend the appearance and manner of utilization of tools which are rare today. One of the main reference books for the area describes a herring rake as being made of cedar, "about twelve inches long with pointed pegs of ironwood," and used by the fisherman to toss fish over his shoulder into the canoe. Fortunately, more accurate descriptions of the herring rake can be found, with the length set at from 7′2″ to roughly 13′ and fish caught while the rake is used like a paddle in the water while the fisherman is seated in a canoe. Unfortunately, many other items have not benefited from diligent portrayals in the literature.

Ceremonial objects, which include masks, spirit boards, hand-held dance clubs, carved figures, rattles and dance poles, were more readily collected, although the religions of western Washington were not afforded much attention. In contrast to more utilitarian items, which have become disassociated with their position in precontact culture, some of the religious objects have maintained their association with traditional use. In fact, some native people today feel it to be inappropriate to exhibit religious objects such as power boards. This objection is raised because the precontact religion, in a somewhat revised form, still persists.

The native people of western Washington were divided into five ethnic/linguistic divisions: the

Left: Puget Sound Camp. Edward Curtis.

Wakashan (the Makah of the Cape Flattery area), Chemakuan (the Chimakum and Quileute of the northern Olympic Peninsula), Athabaskan (the Willapa or Kwalhiokwa of the Willapa Hills), Penutian (the Chinook of the Columbia River area) and Salishan people. The Salish, by far the dominant group of the region, controlled the entire area from the crest of the Cascades to Puget Sound, all the islands of Puget Sound and northward, and the territory to the south and west.

The region was subdivided into coastal, riverine and inland peoples, whose different lifestyles focused on special economic tasks to secure their food resources. Coastal people hunted whales and seals, caught bottom fish and collected shellfish. They also engaged in a more elaborate ceremonial life than did their upriver neighbors. People living upriver or on lakeshores fished for salmon and trout, and hunted ducks. Inland people dug roots, hunted deer, elk and black bear; those on prairies readily adapted to the introduction of the horse and developed a culture surrounding it.

The people in the tribes of western Washington did not rely on chance for finding their raw materials. Specialists knew precisely when and where to gather and hunt in their own neighborhood, and there was an elaborate trade network for gaining materials from distant areas. As with food plants, there were certain seasons for gathering vegetal fibers; conditions such as weather, elevation and amount of sunlight influenced the time when a particular plant was ready to be harvested. Men who worked with stone had particular stretches of river where they located the proper kind of stone.

The cedar tree was perhaps the prime source of raw materials for the Indians of Western Washington. Its bark was beaten and shredded for clothing, its wood was excellent for carving, and its roots were used for watertight baskets and rainhats. Tools, such as adzes, wedges and digging sticks, that necessarily needed to be of harder material than cedar were made of a hardwood, such as yew, or of stone; tribes along the Pacific coast also employed whale bone.

European-made metal and glass was readily integrated into the western Washington cultures, especially by the saltwater peoples who had greater contact with maritime traders. These materials can be found in objects ranging from jewelry to knives. One item in the exhibit, a D-adze, contains brass tacks used as decoration.

Worthy of particular attention are objects that were constructed out of more than one category of material. These composite items might consist of part stone and part fiber, or part wood and part bone. For example, some halibut hooks were carved from cedar wood, the blades (often made out of metal in historic times) lashed to the wood with wild cherry bark or cedar root. Dolls made as toys, or later as sale items, often combined carving, basketry or weaving techniques for the figure portion with clothing made from shredded cedar bark.

The objects created by the native peoples of western Washington made full use of their abundant resources and their construction displays a wide range of talents. It is hoped that "Lost Perspectives" will help to kindle an interest in the history of these peoples; that the complexity of their former material culture and ceremonial life can be appreciated.

Nile Thompson

The Tule Gatherers. Edward Curtis.

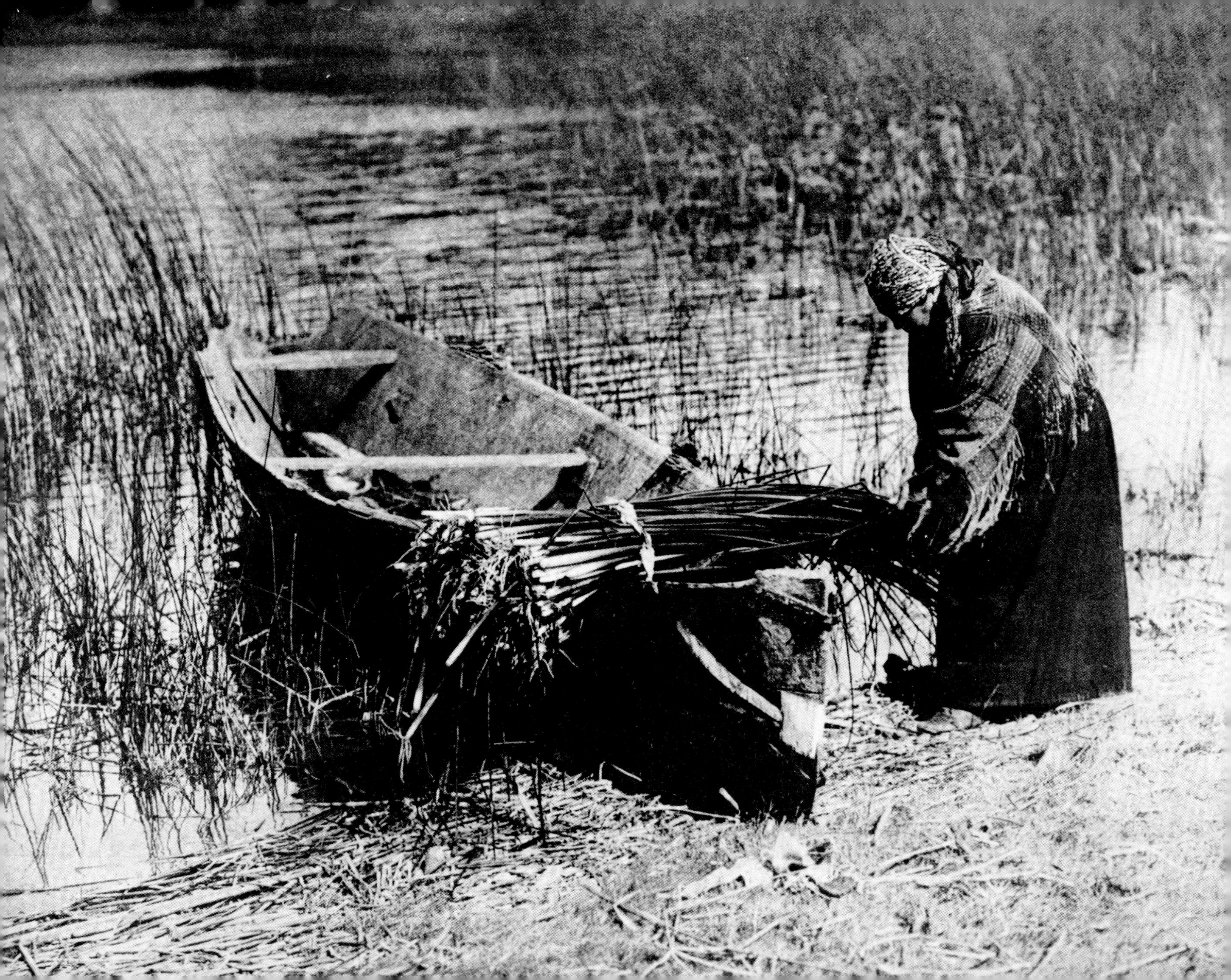

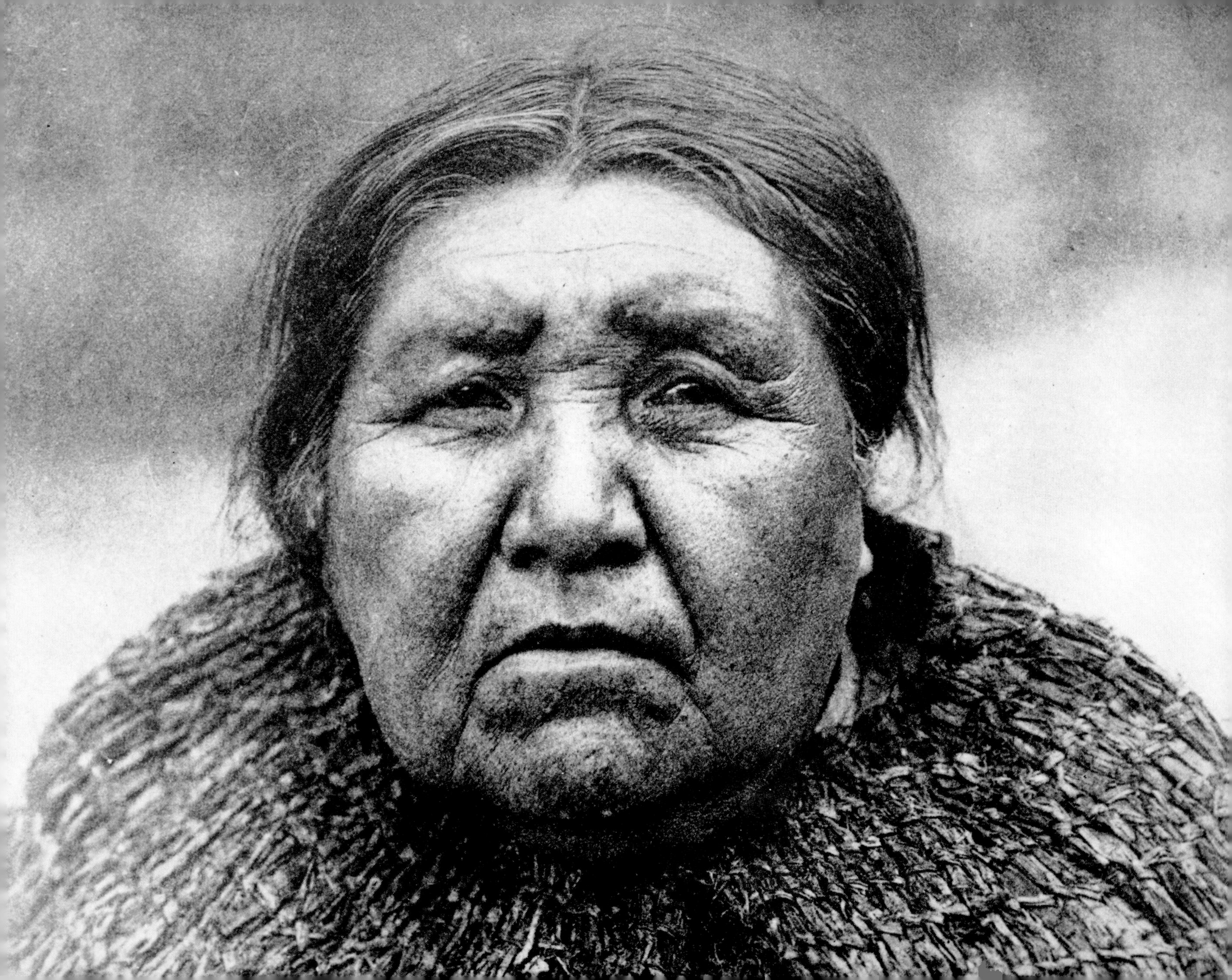

CARVED FIGURE
Makah – late 19th century
Collection of Jerrie and Anne Vander Houwen

Made as a sales item for tourists and collectors. This little lady, nursing her child, illustrates the traditional dress code of earlier times.

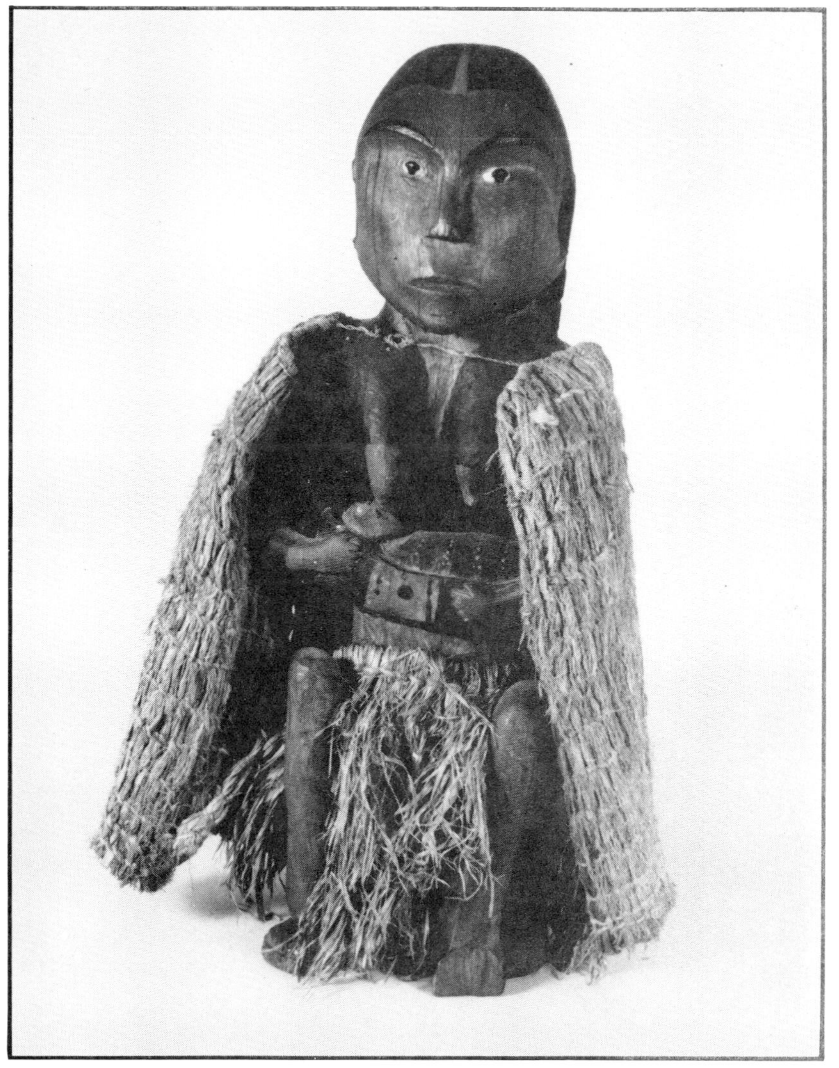

Left: Yalqablu-Skokomish. Edward Curtis.

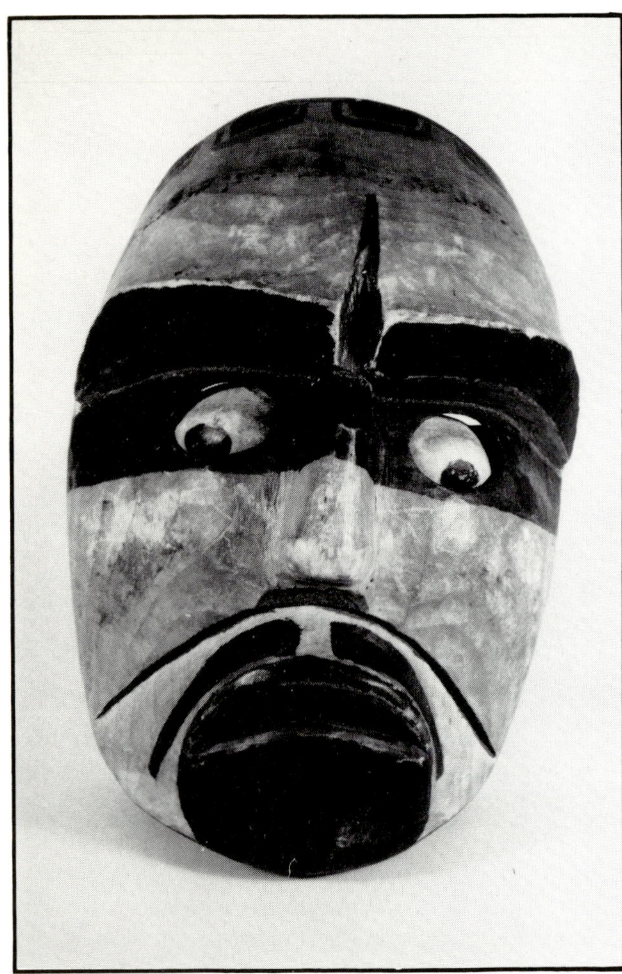

MASK
Makah – mid to late 19th century
Alder
Collection of W.S.H.S.

Used by dancers to dramatize the story being told. This mask is unusual for a Makah mask in that it has moveable eyes.

CARVED POST
Lummi – mid 19th century
Cedar
Collection of W.S.H.S.

This Sxwaixwe post was used in ceremonies connected with the rites of puberty, marriage, name giving, funerals and other very important social events. The carving does not represent any mythical being but is a cleansing instrument.

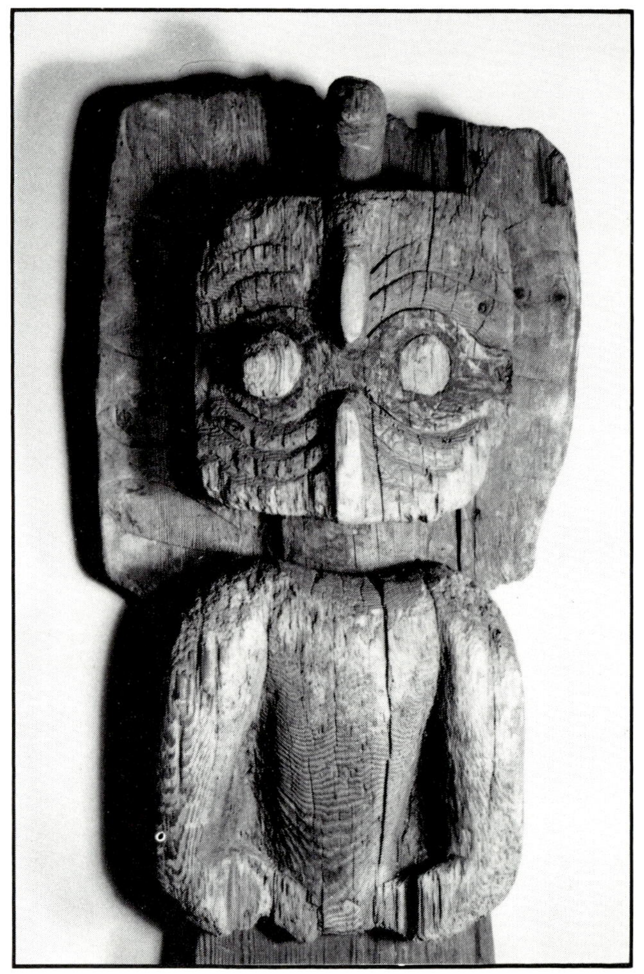

MASK
Makah – mid to late 19th century
Alder
Collection of W.S.H.S.

Worn by dancers to dramatize different spirits associated with Winter Ceremonials. Such masks could represent human forms or mythical ancestors.

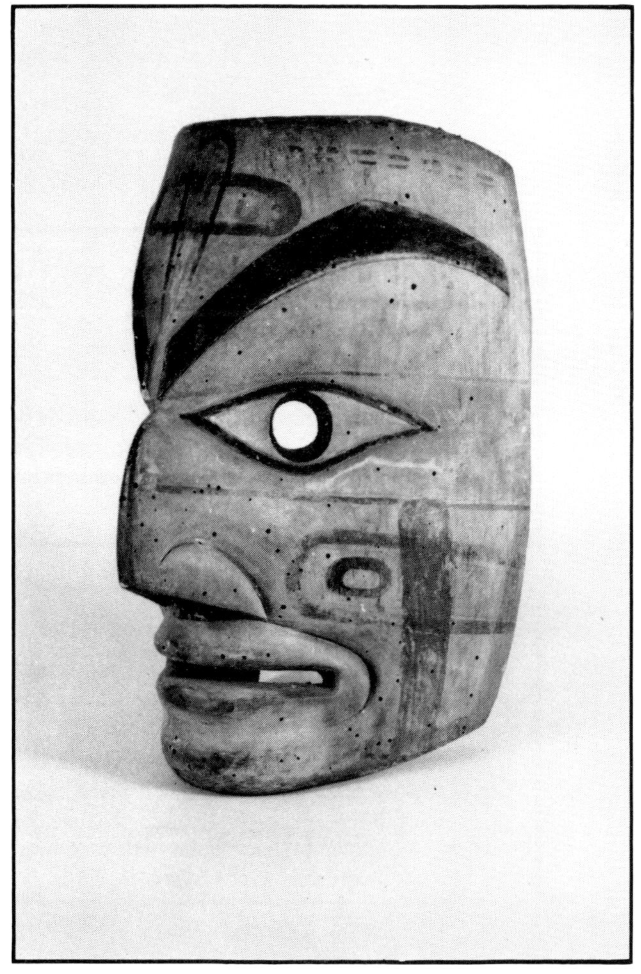

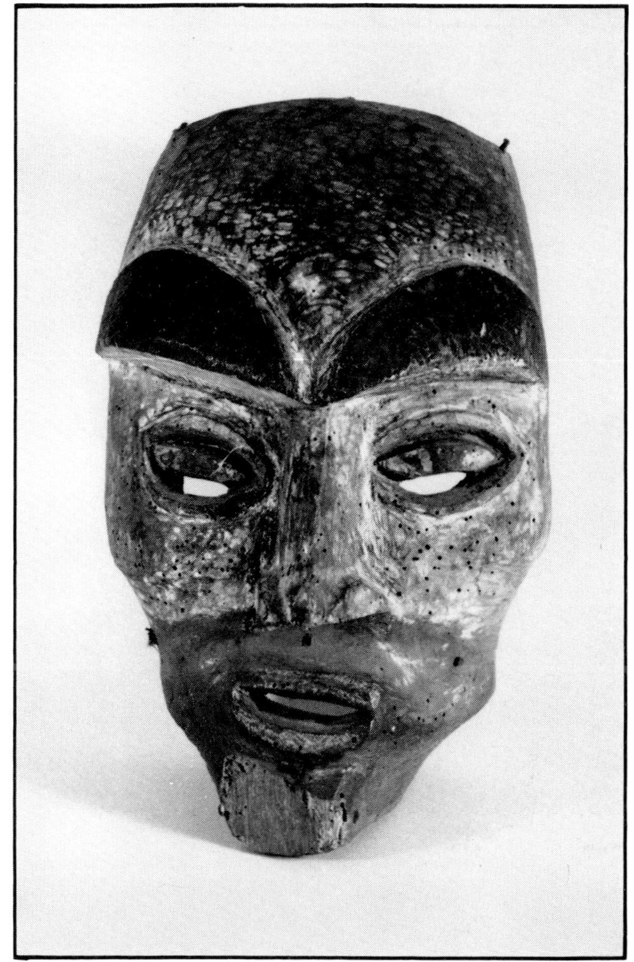

MASK
Makah – late 19th century
Alder
Collection of W.S.H.S.

Used in the winter ceremonies, this mask depicts the human face. The forehead, eyes, nose, and mouth are distorted so that the mask makes more of an impact upon the audience.

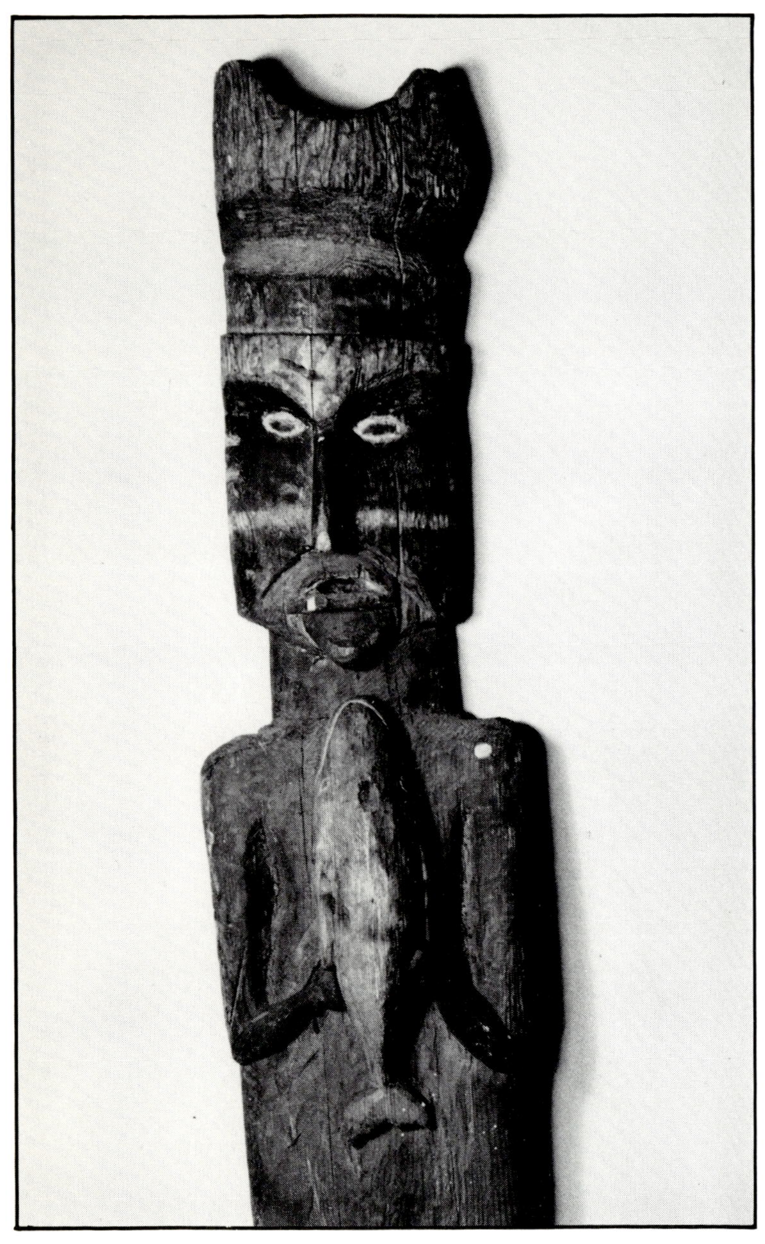

INTERIOR HOUSE POST
Puget Sound — mid to late 19th century
Cedar
Collection of the W.S.H.S.

The interior roof supporting posts of a dwelling sometimes were decorated with carved figures. In the Puget Sound region, the human figure was often used.

CARVED TAMANOUS FIGURE
Nisqually — early 20th century
Cedar
Collection of W.S.H.S.

This 5′7″ carved wooden figure was made by Nisqually Medicine Man, Luke, who was a follower of the celebrated Leschi. He used this figure in power ceremonials dealing with water.

MODEL TOTEM POLE Far Right
Makah — early 1880's
Alder
Collection of W.S.H.S.

Collected by James Swan at Neah Bay in 1882, this pole depicts the thunderbird, killer whales, and grizzly bear. Model poles were made because of the interest created by the large poles of the northern regions, and were sold to collectors.

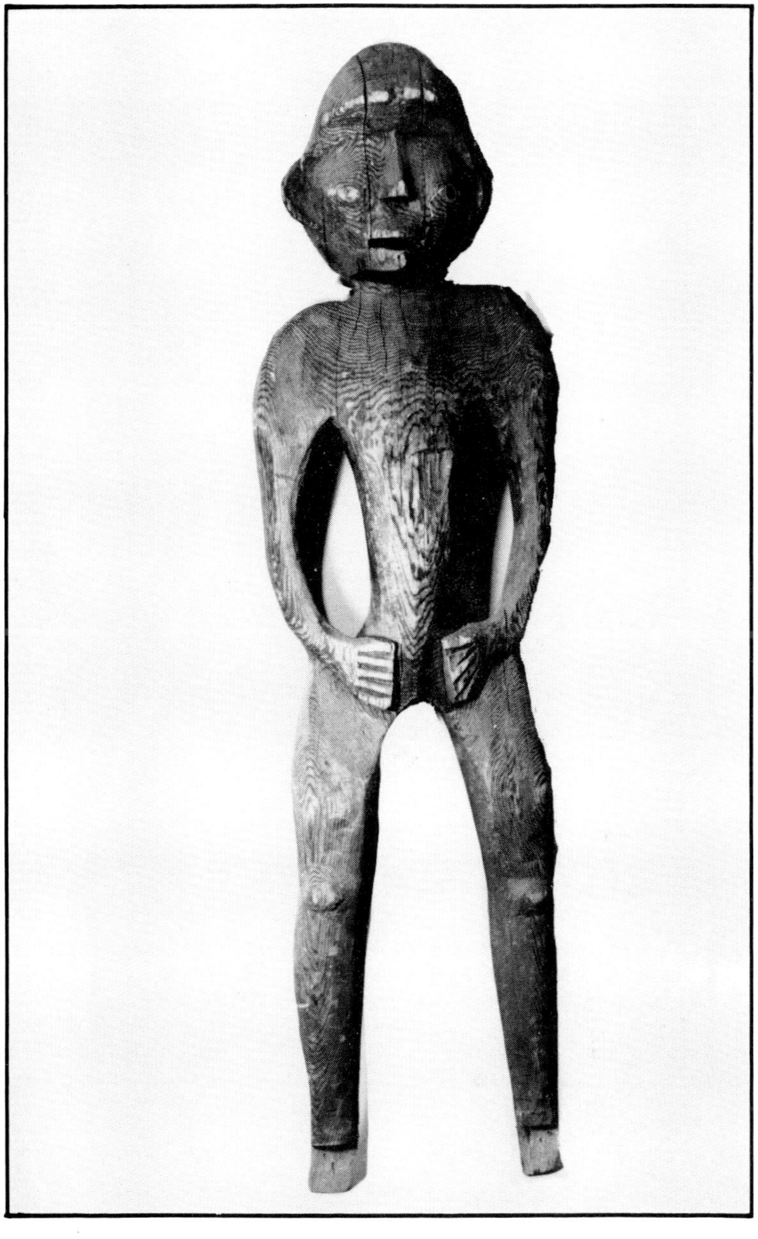

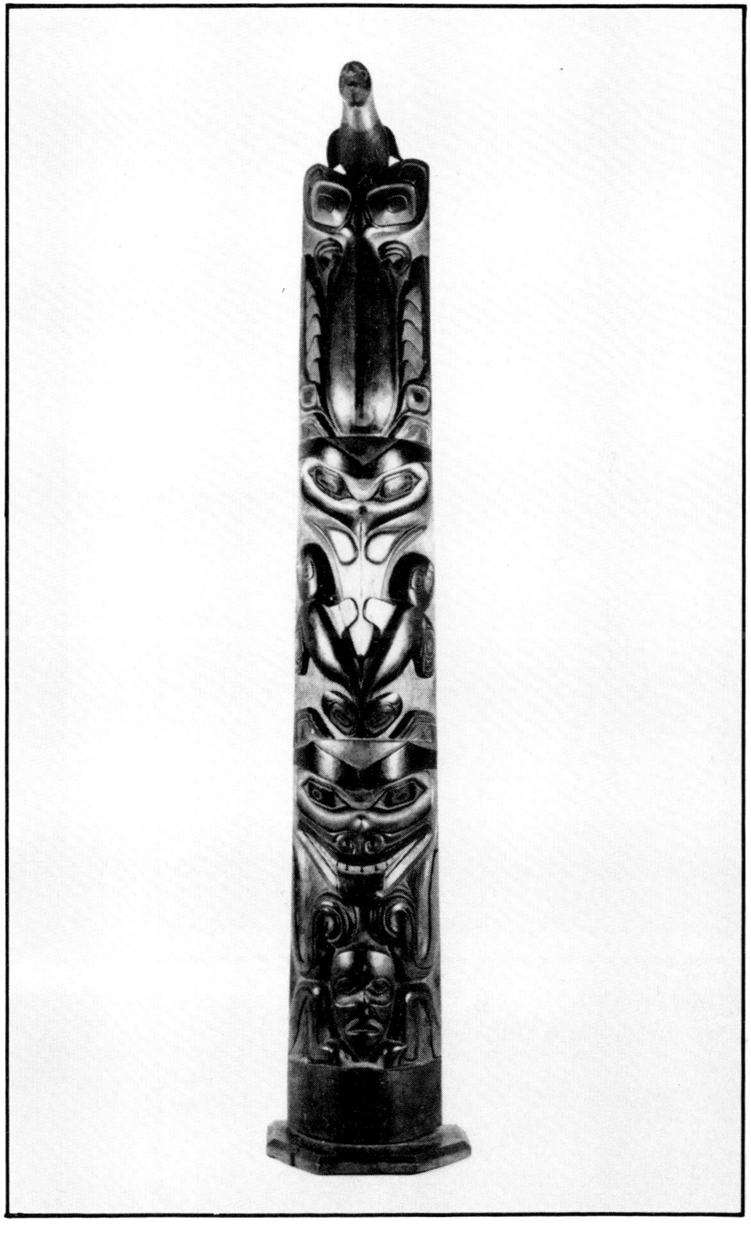

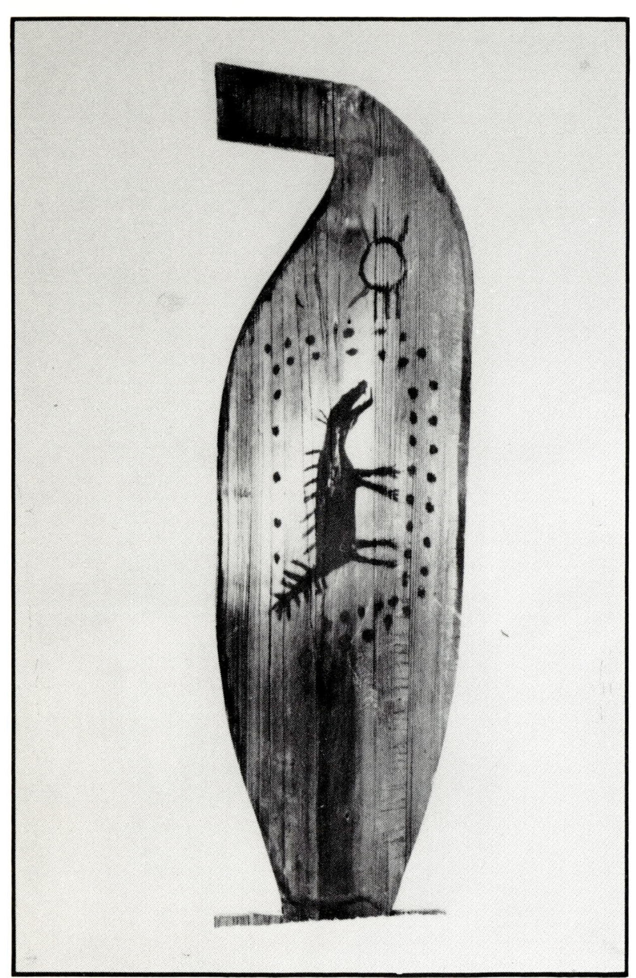

SPIRIT BOARD
Duwamish – late 19th century
Cedar
Collection of W.S.H.S.

Used in the "Spirit Canoe" ceremony which shamans dramatize a trip to the underworld to recover a lost soul or a guardian spirit. This ceremony is unique to the Puget Sound region.

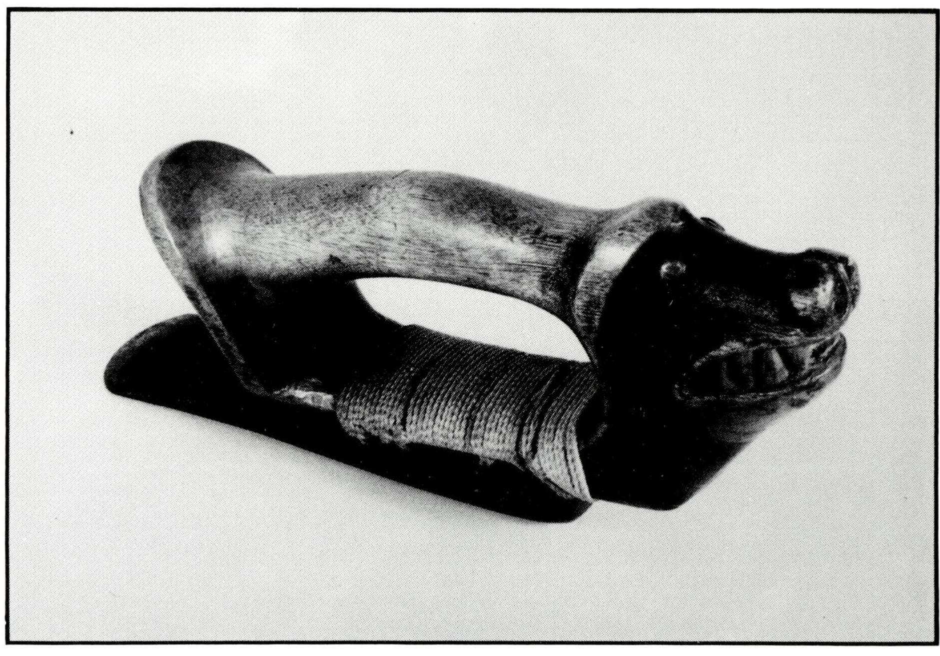

D-ADZE
Coastal – late 19th century
Yew, metal, hemp string, brass tacks
Collection of W.S.H.S.

This tool was used in carving everything from wooden masks, planks and clubs to canoes. The rippled surfaces of adze pocking was regarded as ornamental in itself. The carved face on this adze represents the wolf.

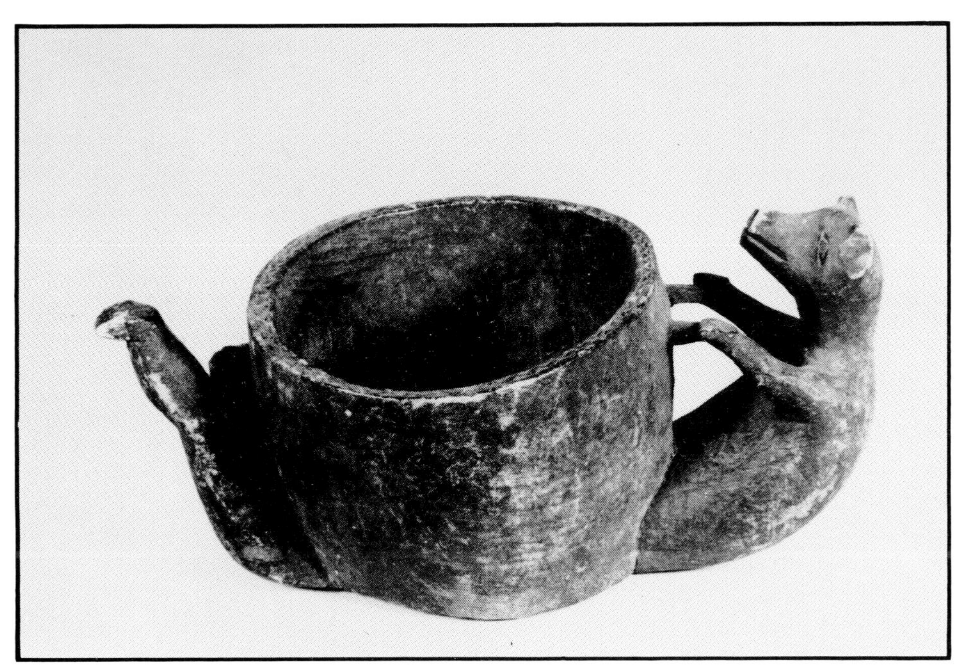

BOWL
Makah – mid 19th century
Cedar
Collection of Delbert J. McBride

This food bowl was used on special occasions or feasts. The animal represented on this bowl is the bear.

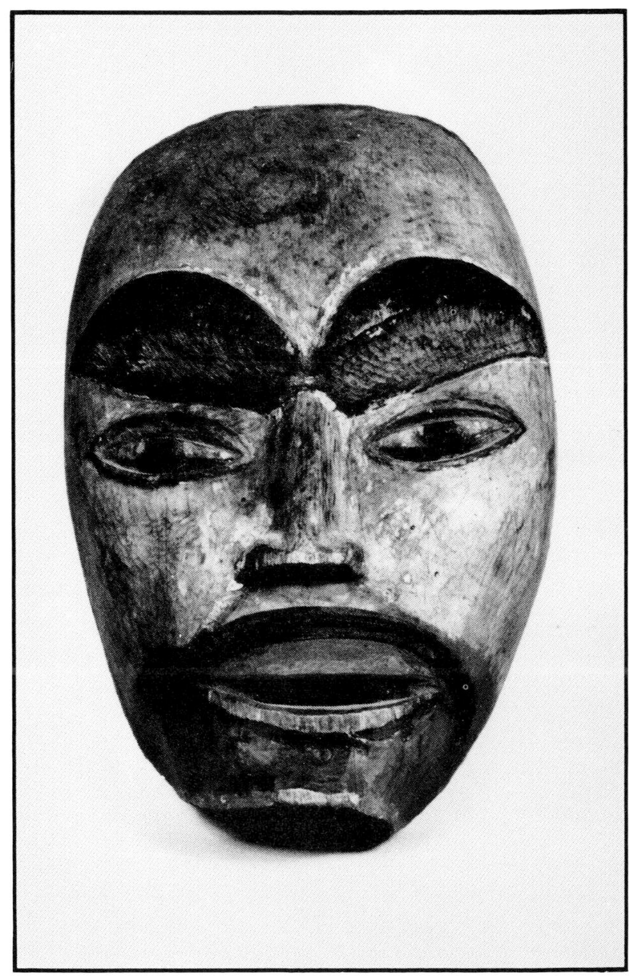

MASK
Makah – mid to late 19th century
Alder
Collection of Mel Marquis

This human mask was used in the winter ceremonials. The bold forehead, nose, mouth and slotted eyes make this a very distinctive mask.

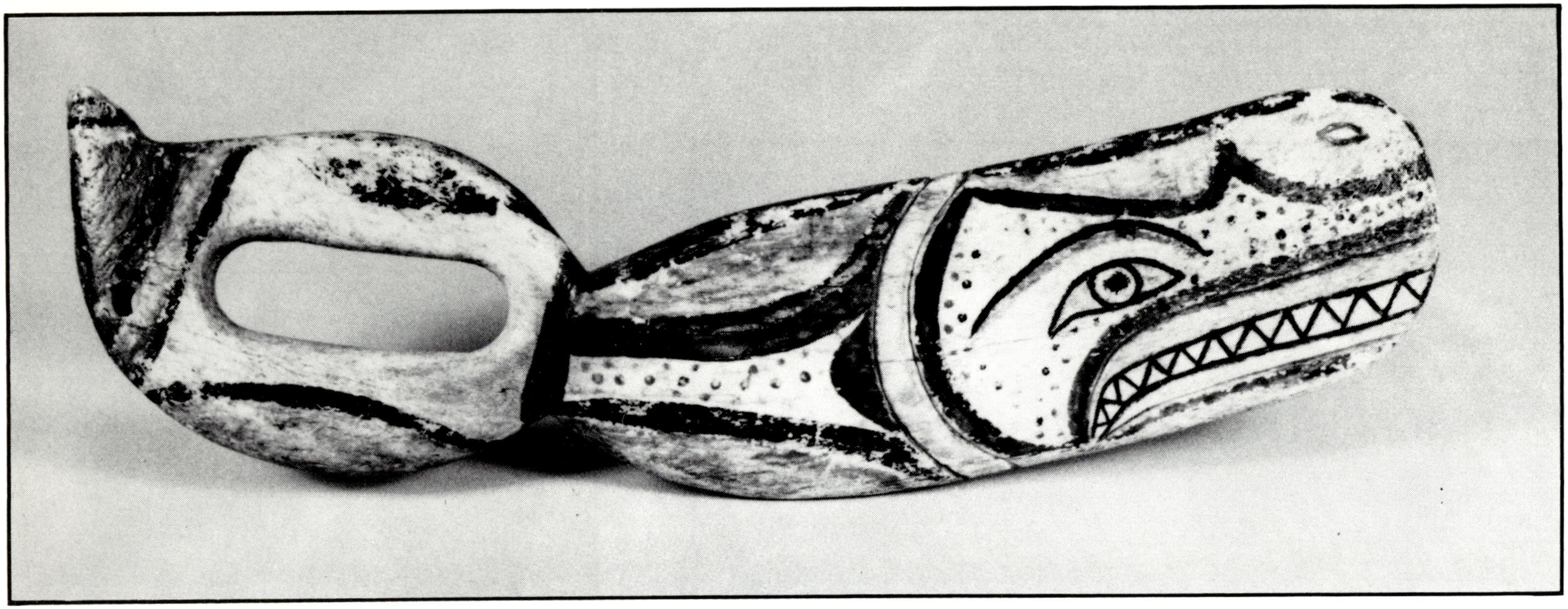

CLUB
Makah — early 20th century
Whalebone
Collection of W.S.H.S.

Rather an unusual piece in that the club is shaped in the form of a whale and the handle is incorporated into the whale's tail. Used to kill larger type fish.

CLUB
Makah — early 20th century
Alder
Collection of W.S.H.S.

These clubs were used to give the death-blow to seals, sea-otters, or fish after their capture. The carved design could be a dog but the long painted ears suggest the carving is of the wolf.

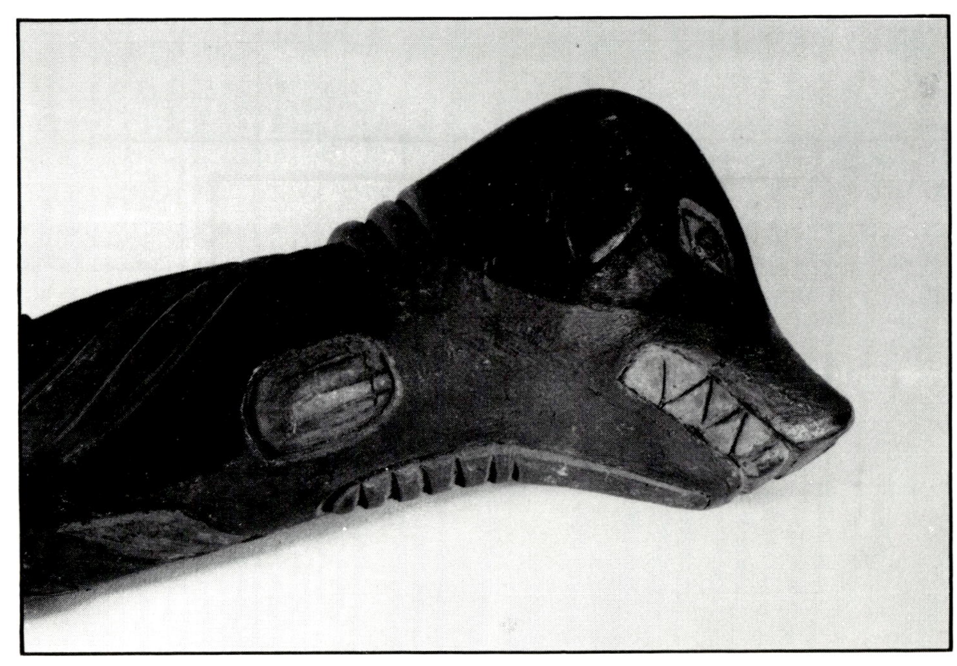

CLUB PORTION
Ozette – 16th century
Whalebone
Collection of Makah Research and Cultural Center

Excavated from the Ozette Archaeological site, this upper portion of a club depicts the thunderbird. Often called a war club, this style club could also have been used for killing seals and fish.

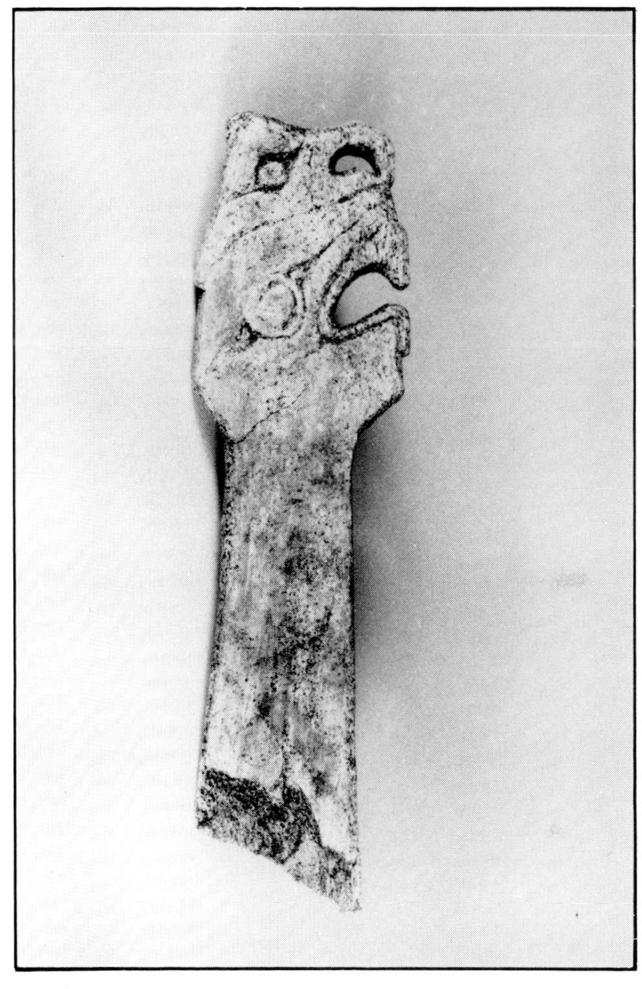

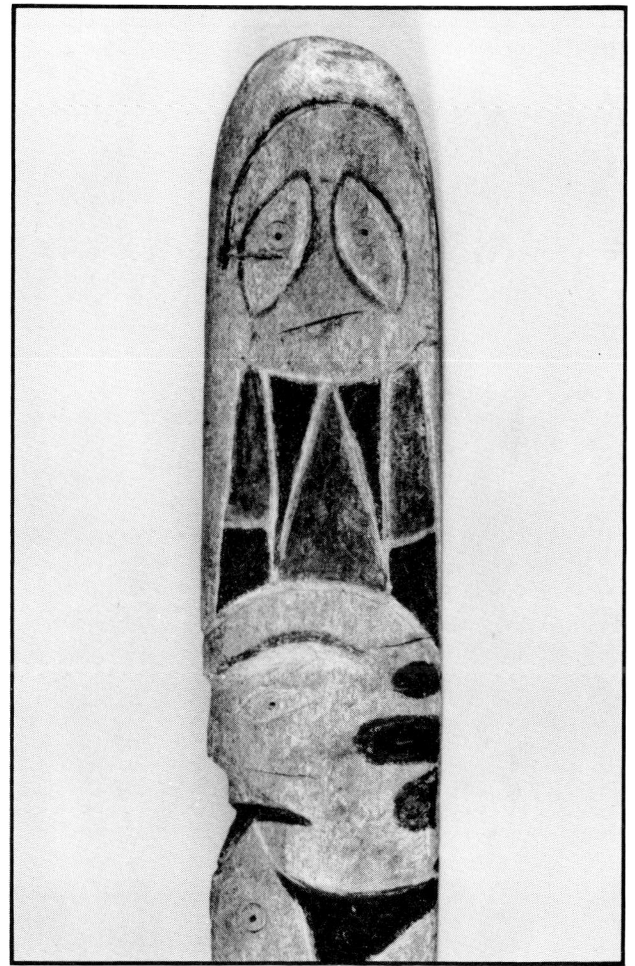

CLUB
Makah – late 19th century
Whalebone
Collection of W.S.H.S.

This club was probably used to kill salmon or other large fish. The design located on upper portion of the club suggests the halibut, while the center portion gives a side view of a human face.

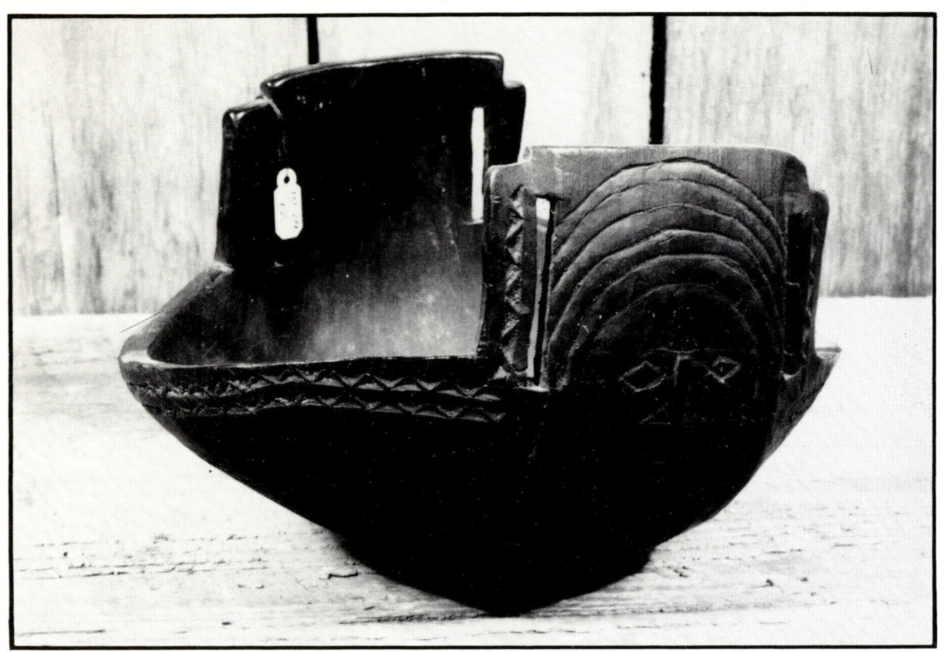

BOWL
Chinook – late 19th century
Mountain-sheep horn
Collection of State Capital Museum

The bowl was made by splitting the horn at its base, softening the horn by steaming it, then shaping it in a wooden mold made up of two pieces. While still soft the carvings were applied.

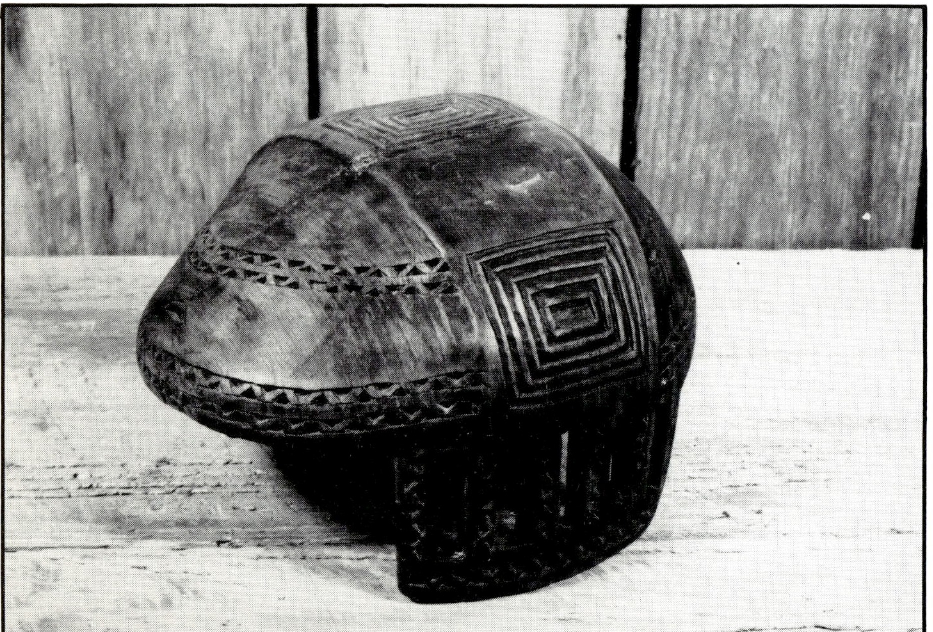

BOWL
Chinook – late 19th century
Mountain-sheep horn
Collection of State Capital Museum

The Chinook carvers became well known for their skill in making the mountain-goat bowls. They placed a high value on them and the bowls became a prized possession to their owners.

HORN LADLE
Chinook – mid 19th century
Mountain-goat horn
Collection of State Capital Museum

Highly decorated spoons such as this one with the dog or wolf figure on the handle were usually reserved for feast use. Goat horn is easily carved while fresh and hardens with age.

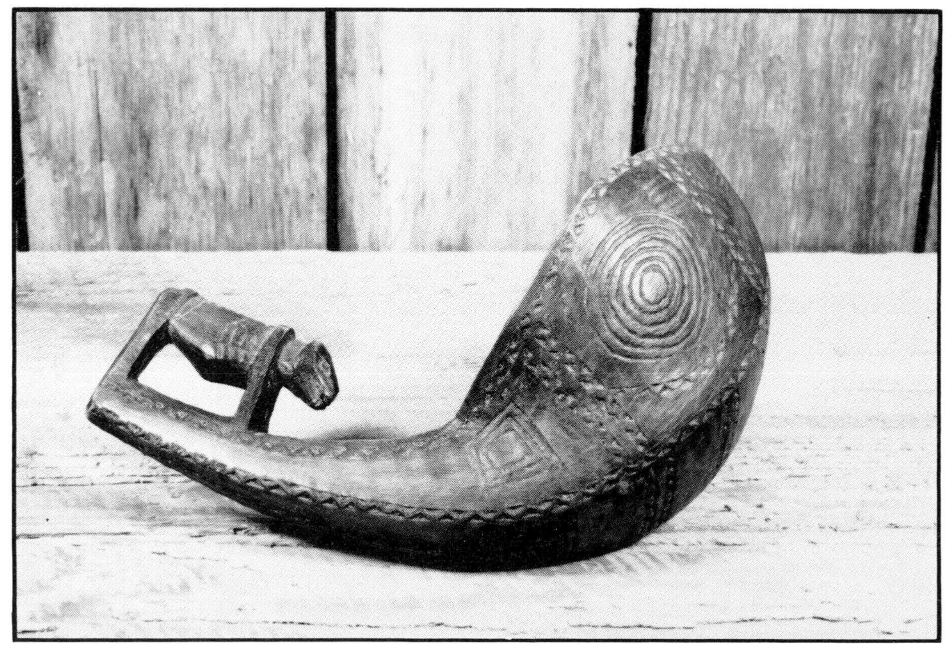

BOX SIDE
Ozette – 16th century
Cedar
Collection of Makah Cultural and Research Center

The side of this bentwood box is interesting because of its carved surface. The center symbol is unknown.

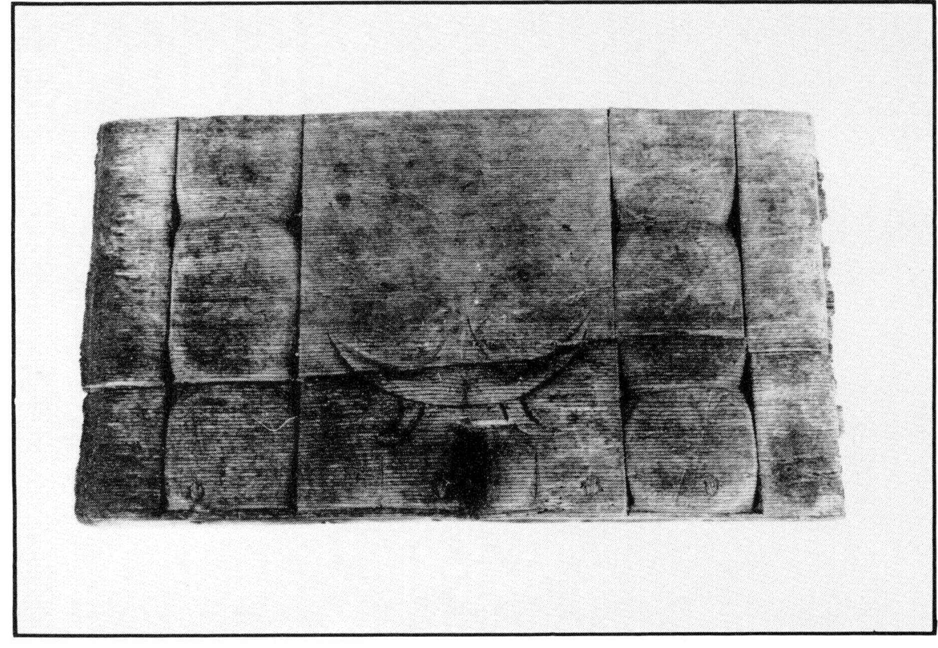

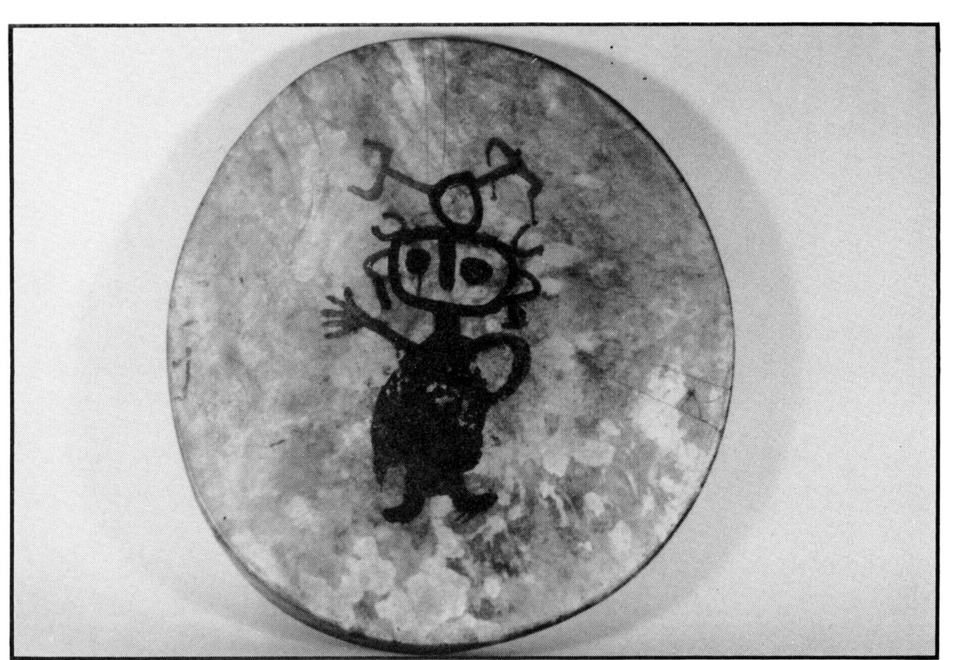

DRUM
Duwamish — late 19th century
Deer skin and cedar
Collection of Jack Curtright

Used during ceremonial dances. The style of the human figure leads one to believe it might have been used during the "spirit canoe" ceremony.

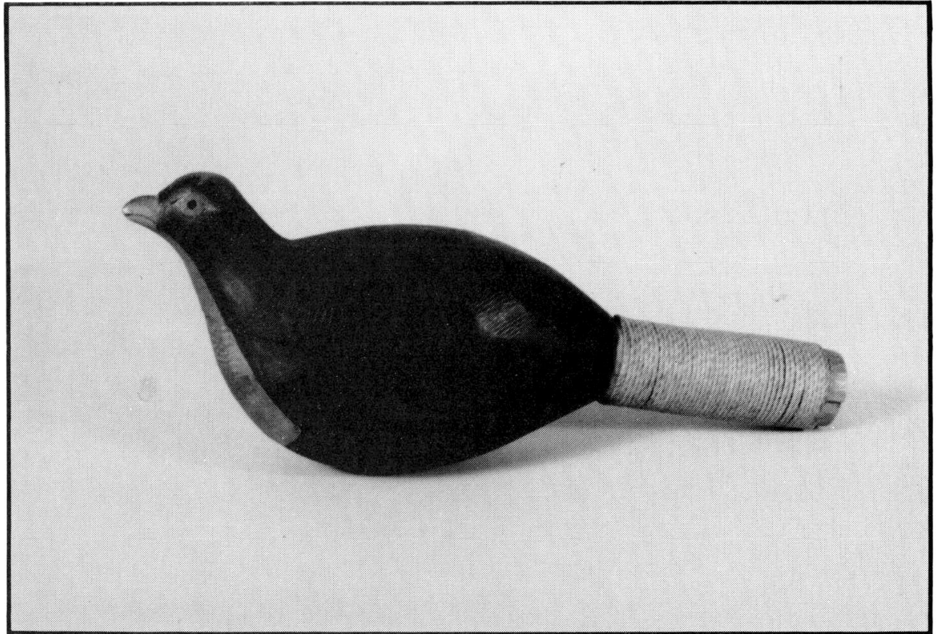

RATTLE
Klallam
Wood, cotton twine
Collection of Jerrie and Anne Vander Houwen

This ceremonial bird rattle, with its plump body and small head, represents a grouse. When carved, the bird was split in half, hollowed out, filled with pebbles, and the two pieces were joined.

HEADBAND
Makah – late 19th century
Dentalium, leather, trade beads
Collection

Traded for from the Nootka Indians of the North, these small white shells were strung into head pieces and necklaces. Usually worn at ceremonies, these dentalium ornaments were a sign of wealth.

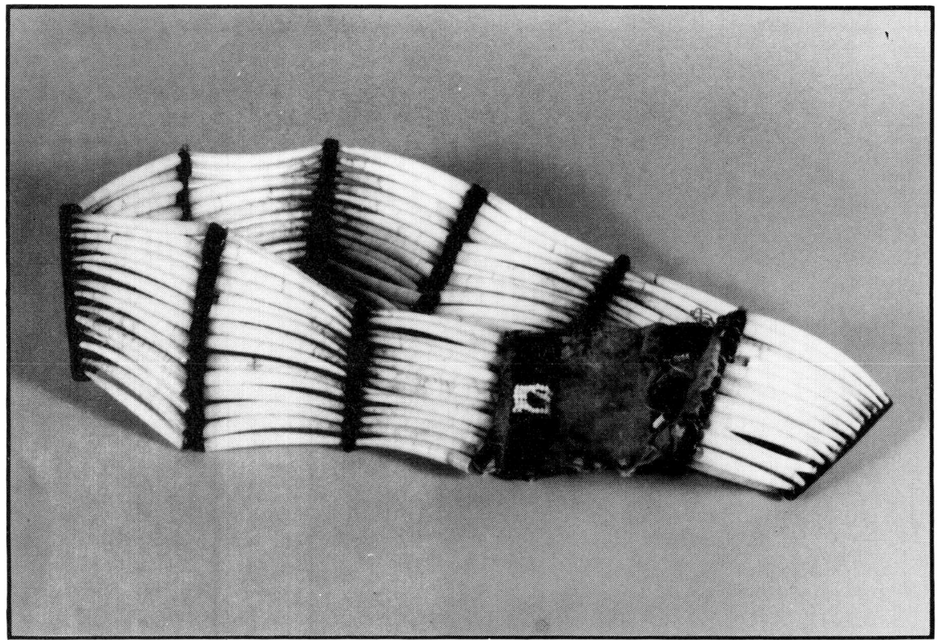

ANCHOR AND ROPE
Chehalis – mid to late 19th century
Stone, cedar bark
Collection of Cowlitz County Historical Society

Possibly used as a canoe anchor. This anchor is unique in that a hole was drilled through the top so that the cedar bark rope could be attached.

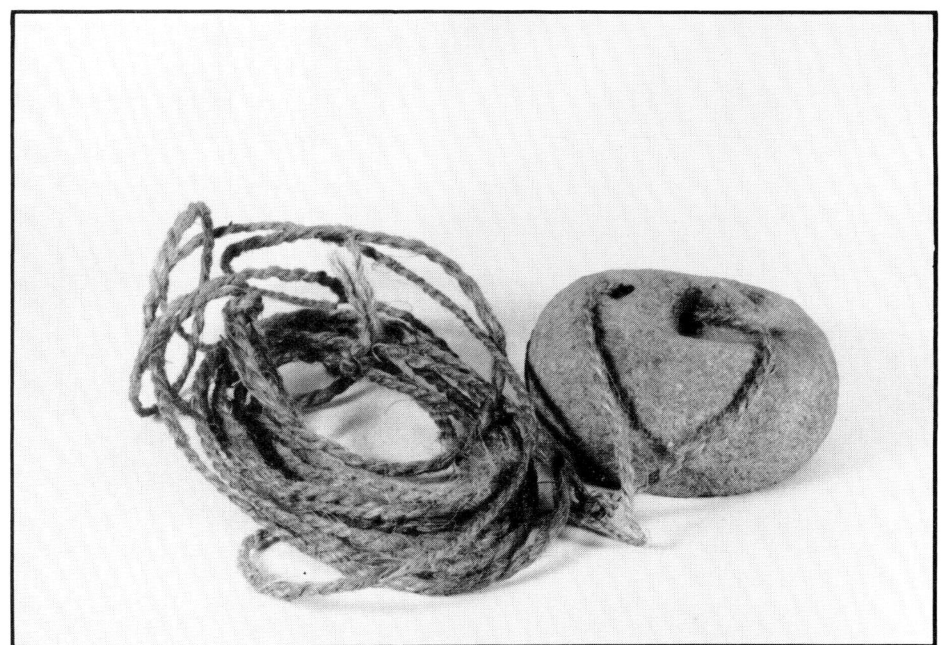

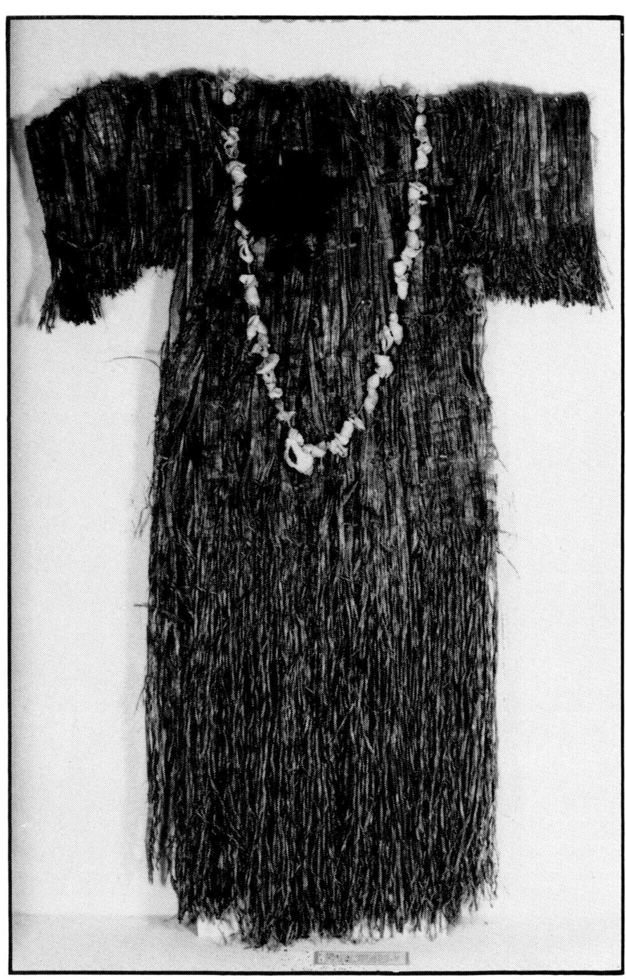

DRESS
Coastal – late 19th century
Cedar bark
Collection of State Capital Museum

Constructed of cedar bark which was soaked in water and then beaten to make it soft and pliable. This style of dress replaced the older style of women's wear which consisted of a cedar bark skirt and cape.

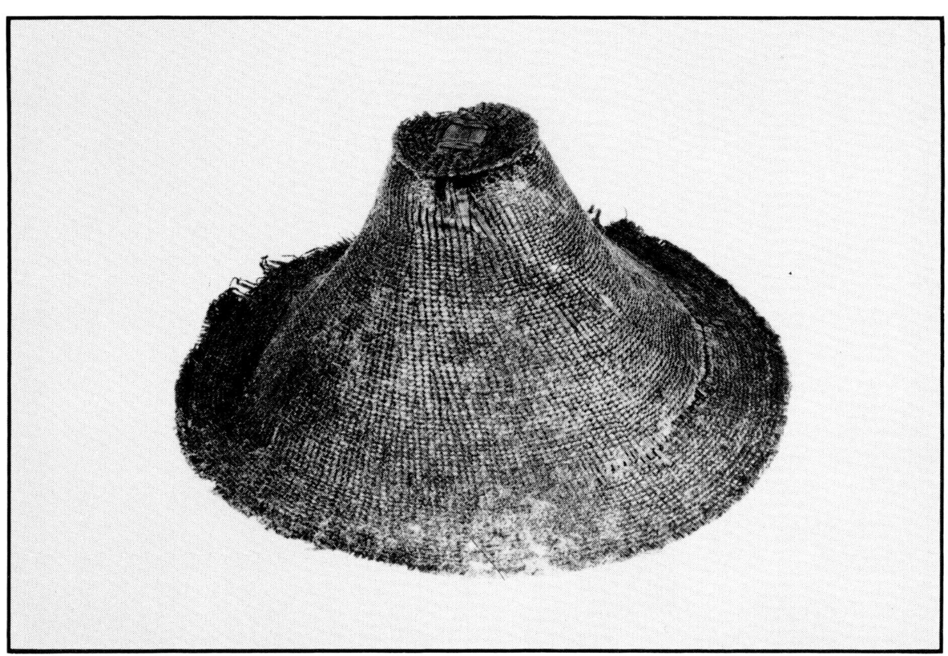

HAT
Ozette – mid 16th century
Spruce root
Collection of Makah Research and Cultural Center

Because of the needs of the people on the rainy coast, the conical woven hat was developed out of the basketry technology. They were only worn on the coast.

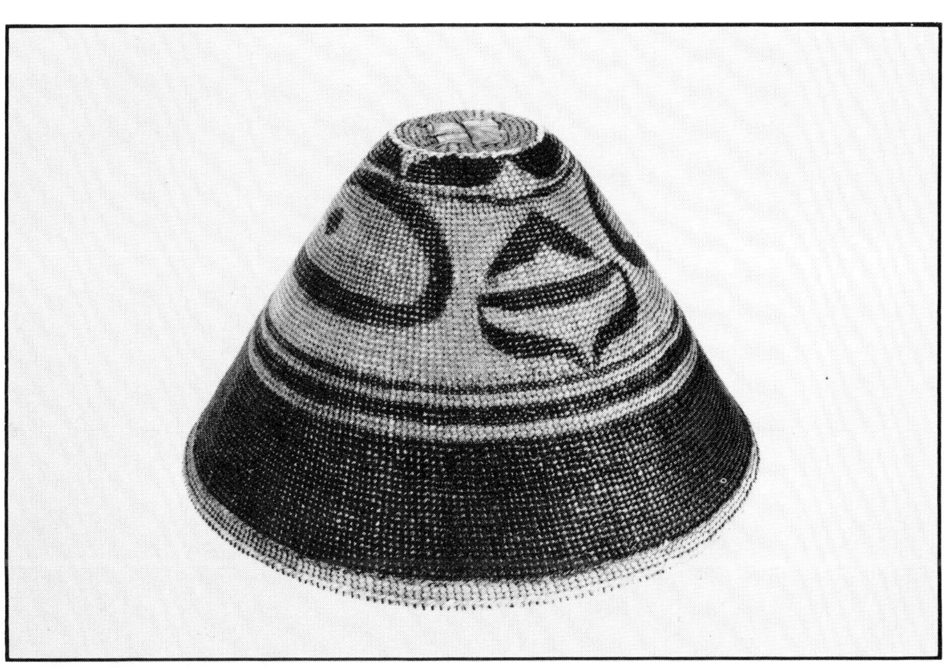

HAT
Makah — late 19th century
Cedar bark
Collection of W.S.H.S.

The domed-shaped hat, twined of red cedar bark, was the most common style of hat found on the Northwest Coast. Often left plain, this hat, however, has been painted with abstract forms.

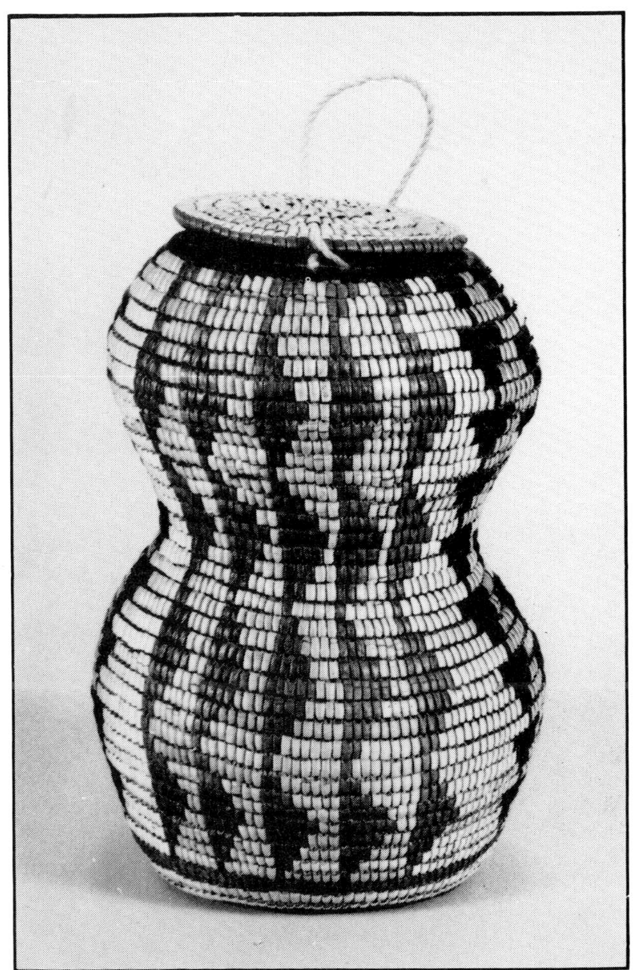

BASKET
Nisqually — mid to late 19th century
Cedar root with beargrass and cedar bark imbrication
Collection of Lee Miner

Unusual shapes were sometimes done to display the skill of the weaver. This non-traditional style basket was made by Si-a-gut and was collected by James Wickersham in 1899.

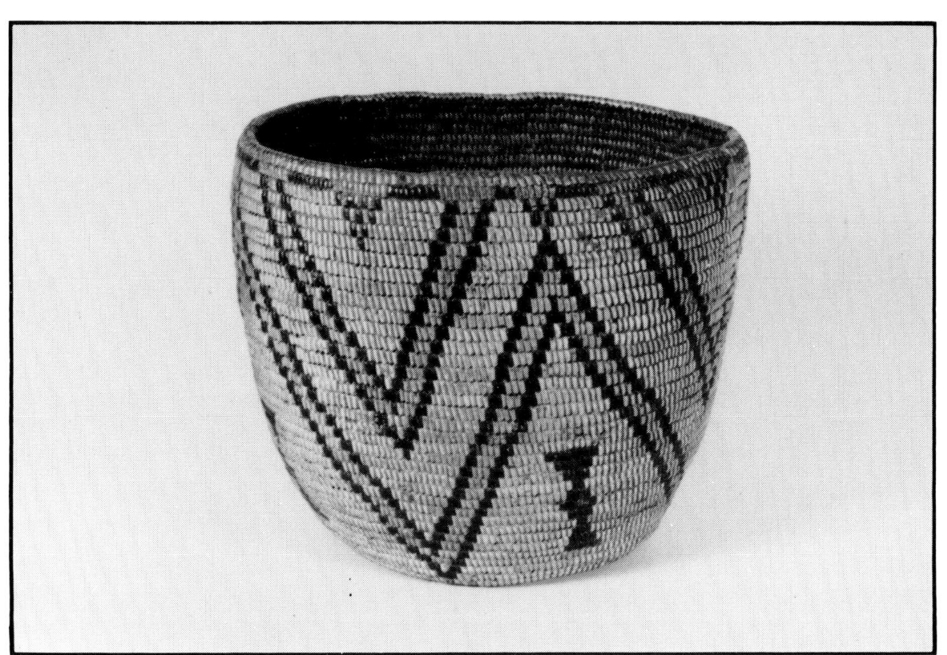

BASKET
Cowlitz—mid 19th century
Cedar with beargrass and cedar bark imbrication
Collection of Jerrie and Anne Vander Houwen

This basket is of exceptionally fine craftsmanship. The mountain was used for the design.

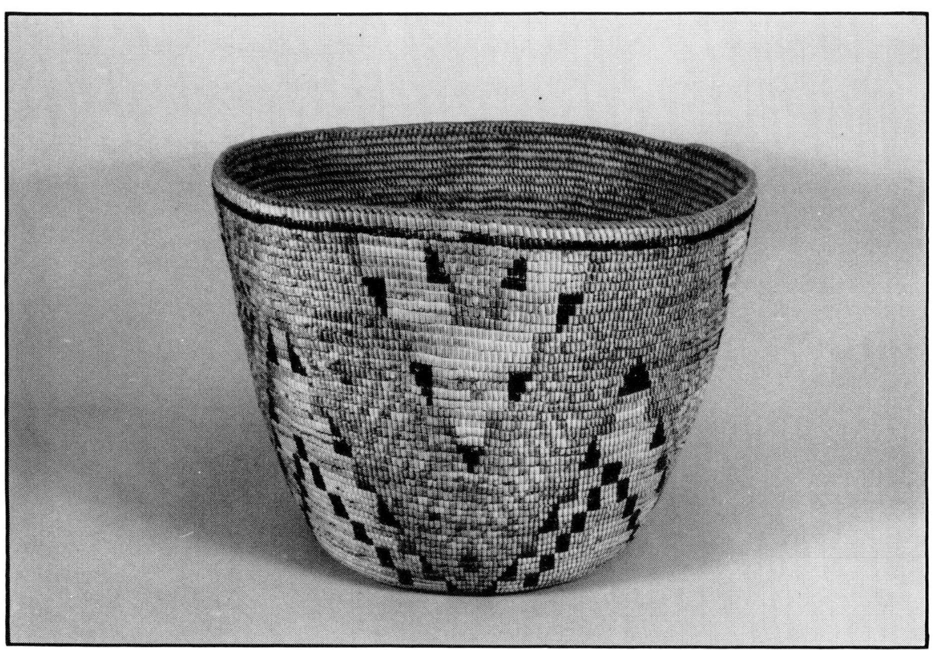

BASKET
Cowlitz—late 19th century
Cedar root with beargrass and cedar bark imbrication
Collection of Lee Miner

This is a typical storage style basket of this time period. The outstanding feature of this basket is the dyed beargrass used in the imbricated design work.

BASKET
Twana – late 19th century
Cattail with beargrass and cedar bark overlay
Collection of Lee Miner

A storage basket for clothing or other soft goods. The design on the main portion is called the seal roost and the animals around the rim are wolves.

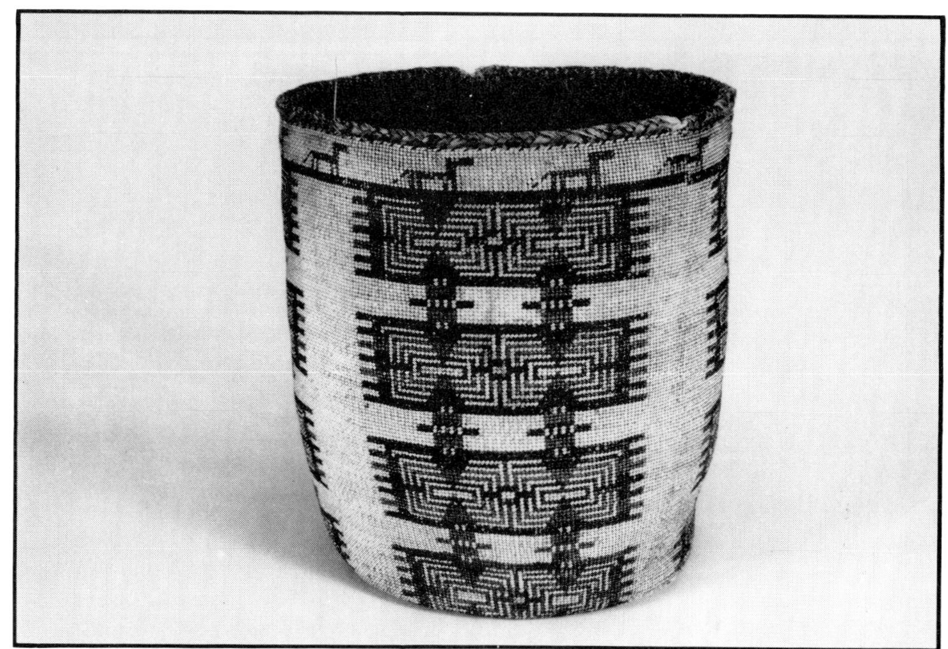

BASKET
Puget Sound – early 19th century
Cedar with beargrass and cedar bark imbrication
Collection of Jerrie and Anne Vander Houwen

This very old basket incorporates a variation of the salmon gill as its decoration.

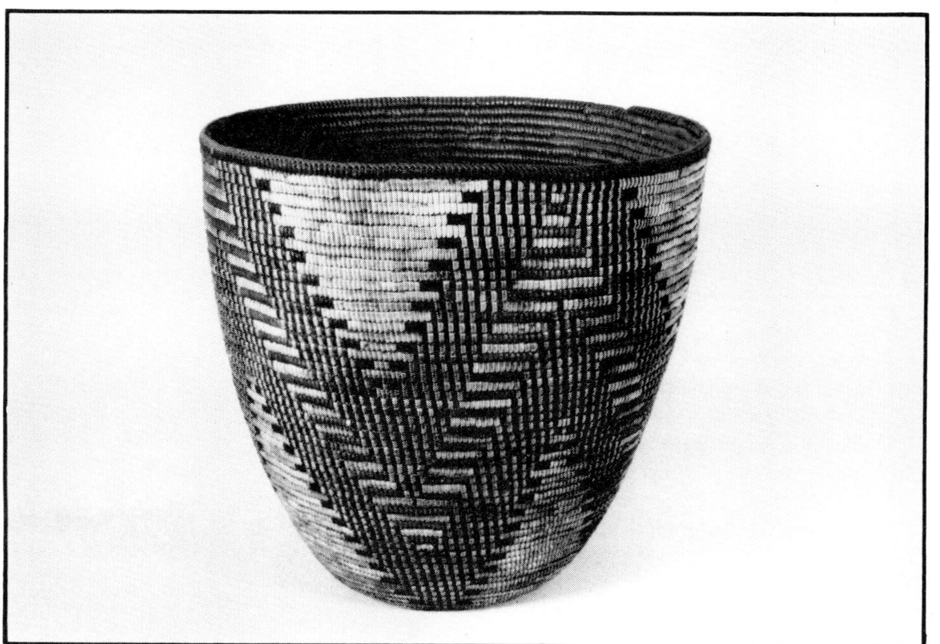

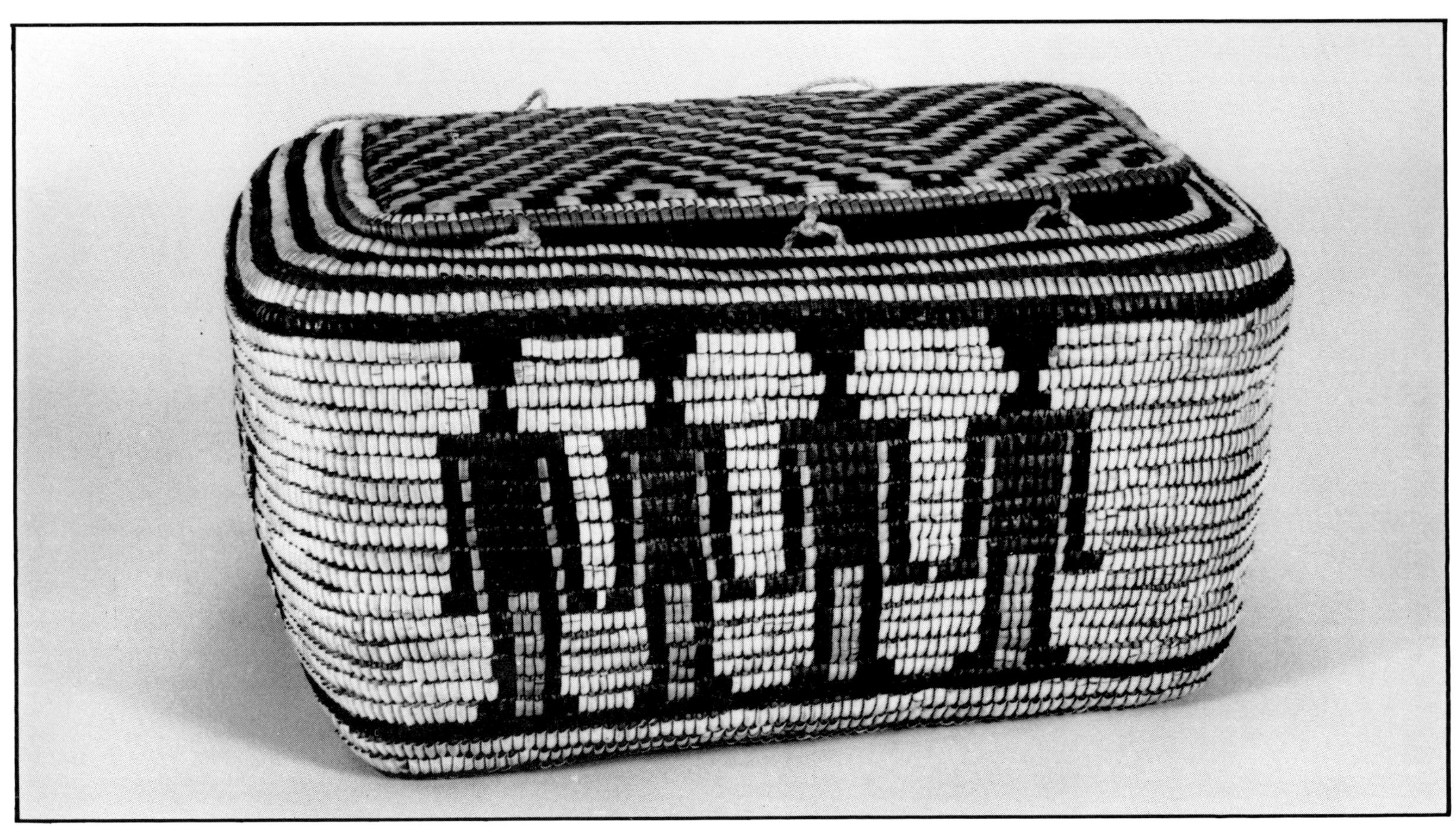

BASKET
Nisqually—mid to late 19th century
Cedar root with beargrass and cedar bark imbrication
Collection of Lee Miner

This basket was woven by Si-a-gut, a Nisqually women who lived on the Upper Nisqually River area. Human figures were one of her favorite designs on her baskets.

BASKET
Skagit – mid to late 19th century
Cedar root with beargrass, cedar bark and wild cherry bark imbrication
Collection of Jerrie and Anne Vander Houwen

This basket is notable because of its reverse color design of having the dark background and light colored design. Used for carrying or storing dry materials such as sewing materials or dried food.

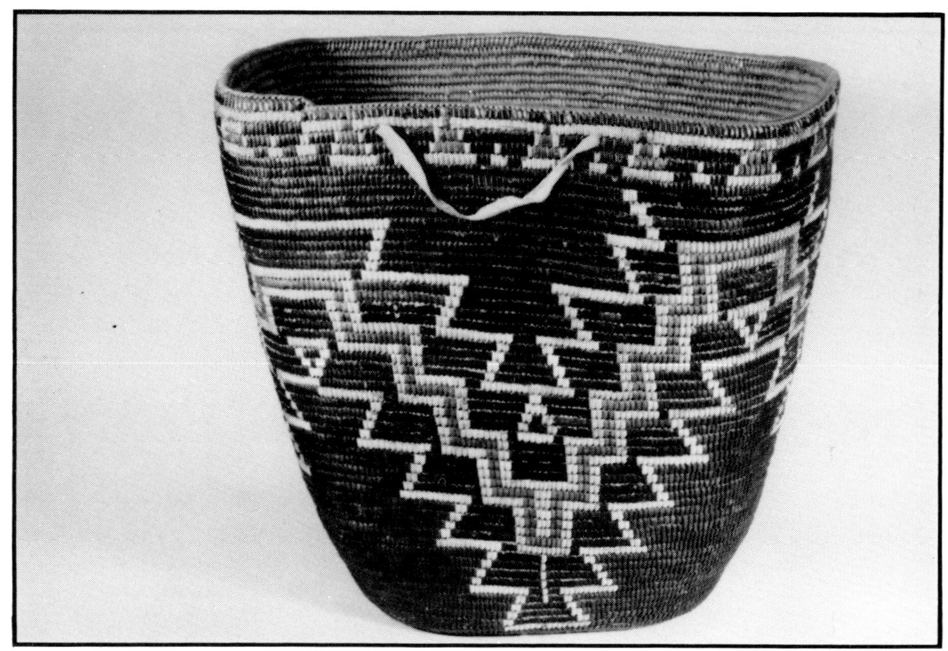

BASKET
Cowlitz – late 19th century
Cedar with beargrass and cedar bark imbrication
Collection of Jerrie and Anne Vander Houwen

The mountain design is used to decorate the main portion of this storage basket.

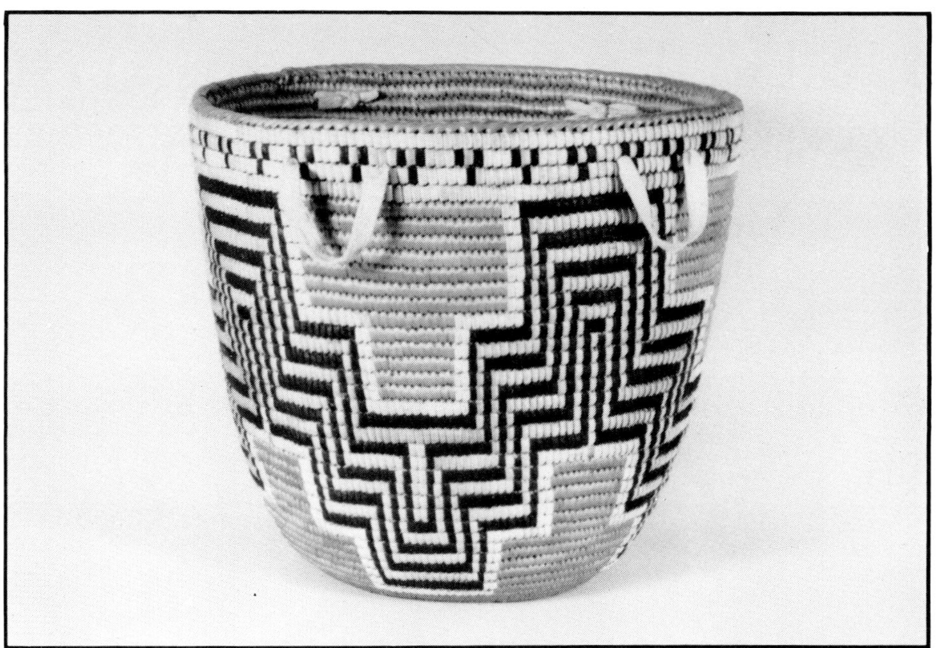

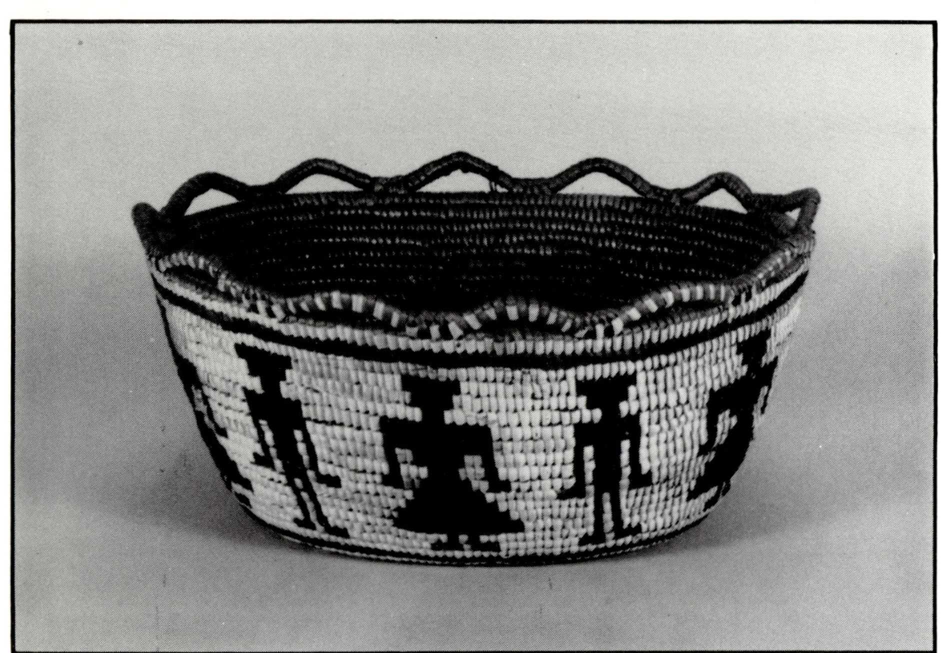

BASKET
Nisqually — mid to late 19th century
Cedar root with beargrass and cedar bark imbrication
Collection of Lee Miner

Si-a-gut made this basket using both the male and female figures as decoration.

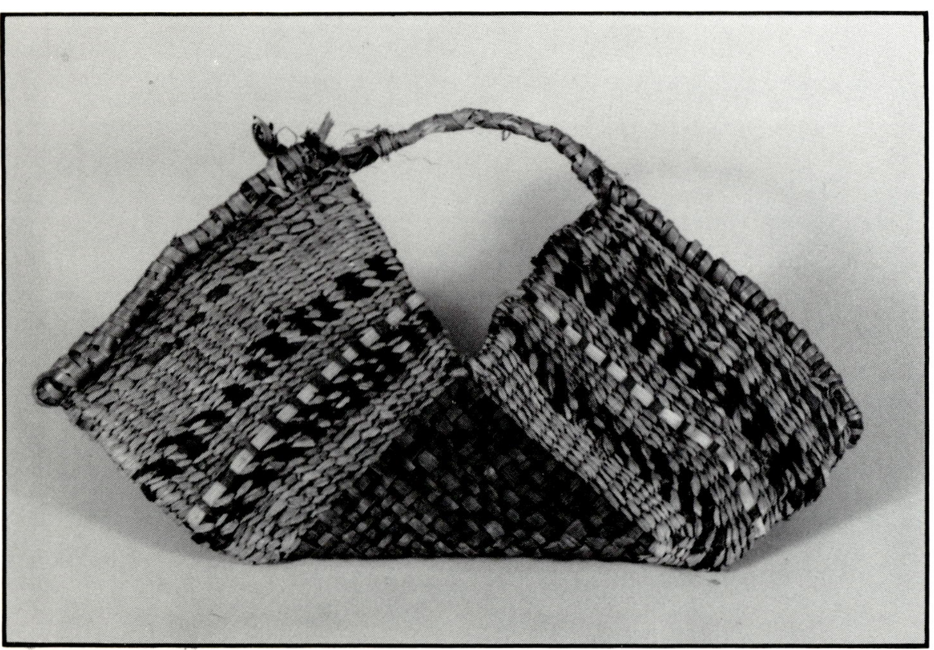

BASKET
Chehalis — early 20th century
Cedar bark, beargrass
Collection of Cowlitz County Historical Society

Commonly called a trinket basket and was made as a sales item. During this time period, Indian women experimented making odd shaped baskets to sell.

BASKET
Cowlitz – late 19th century
Cedar root with beargrass and cedar bark imbrication
Collection of Lee Miner

This hard coiled basket could have been made for the storage of dry goods or it could have been made as a gift item. The basket would be treasured by its owner and act as a sign of wealth.

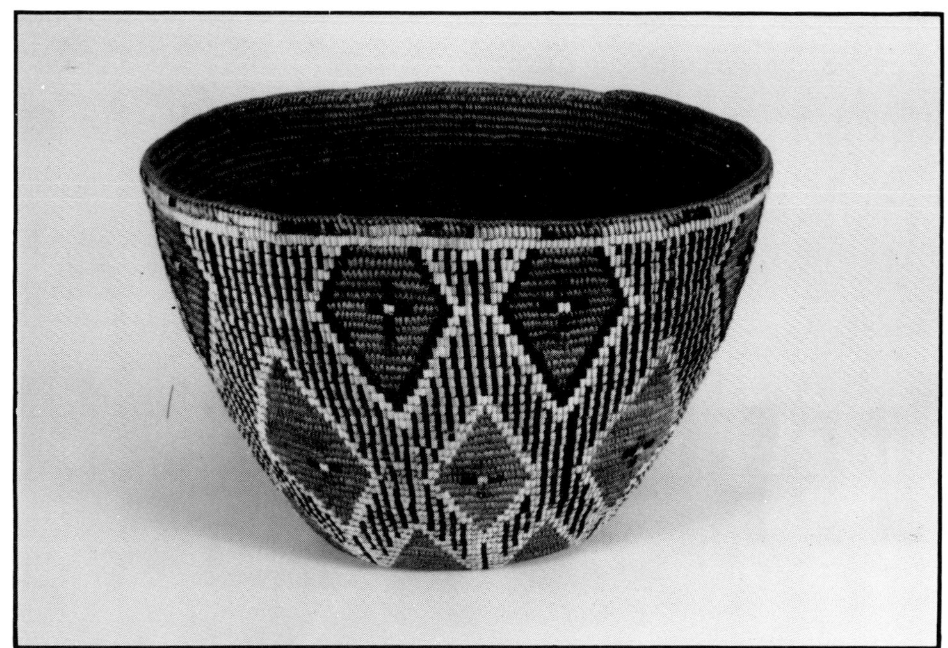

BASKET
Nisqually – mid to late 19th century
Cedar with beargrass and cedar bark imbrication
Collection of Jerrie and Anne Vander Houwen

This fully imbricated basket was made by Si-a-gut and was collected by James Wickersham in 1899.

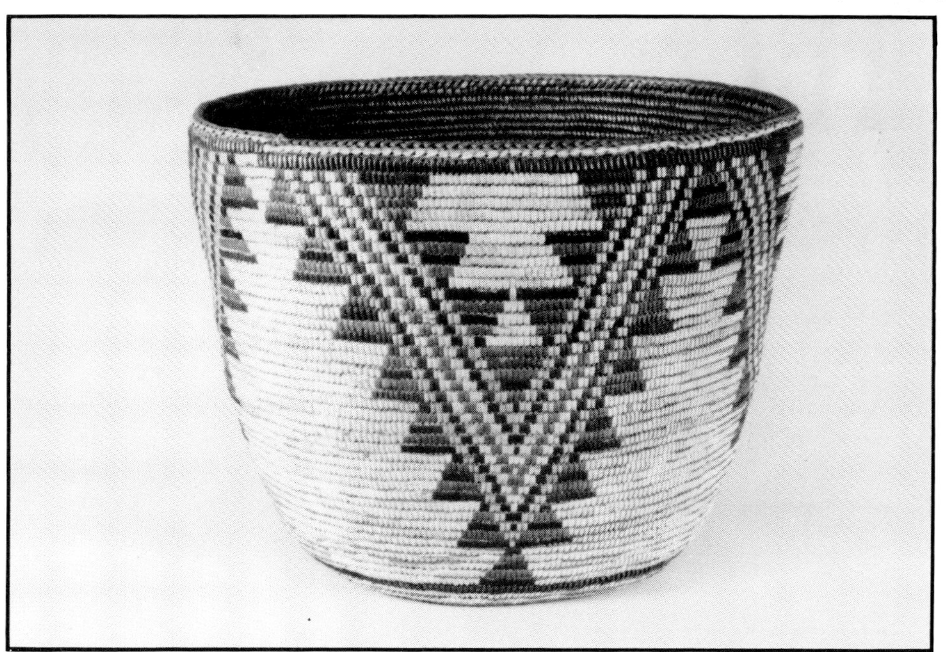

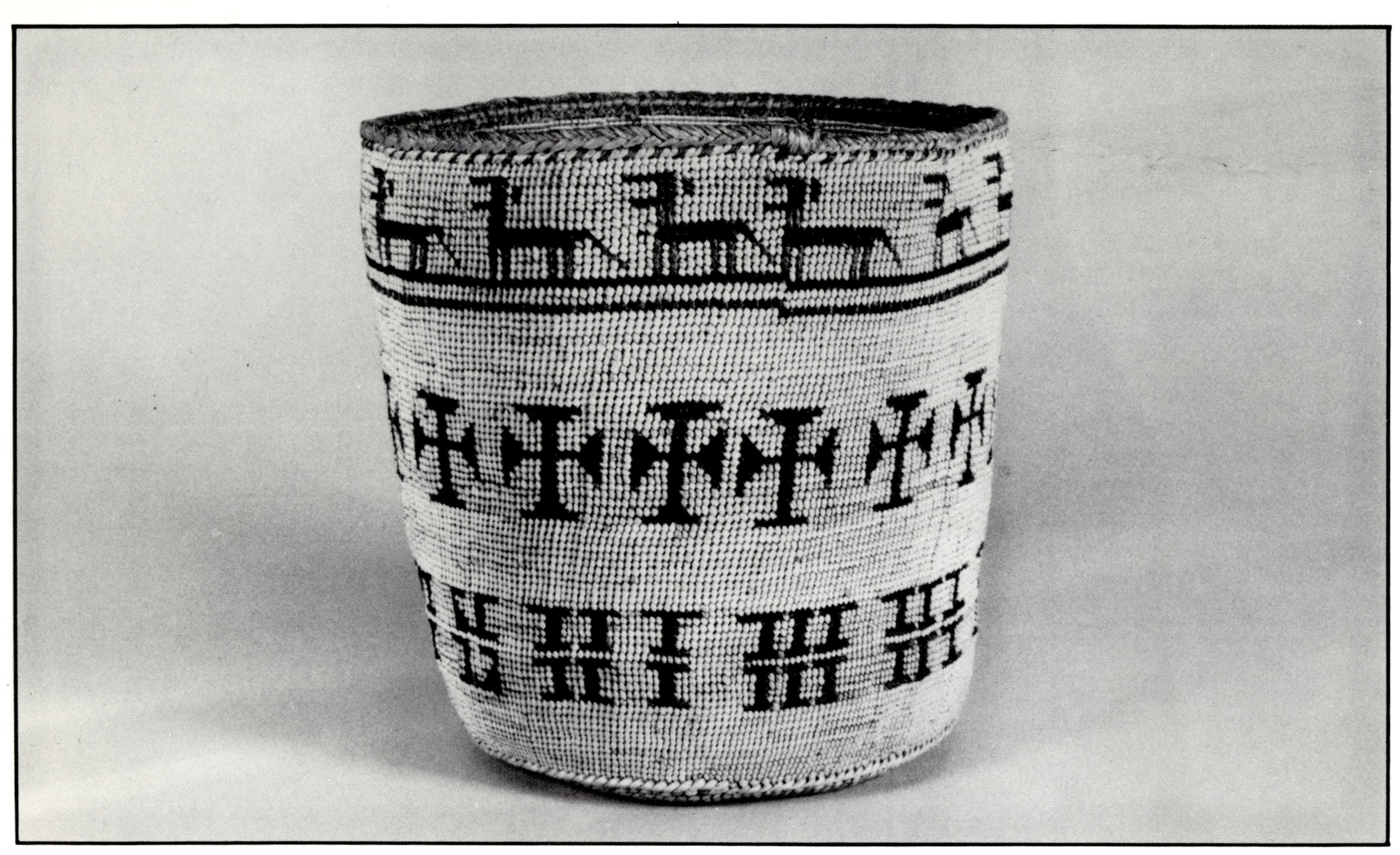

BASKET
Chehalis – mid to late 19th century
Cattail, beargrass and maidenhair fern
Collection of Natalie Linn

Superb example of craftsmanship and technical skill in basketry. Made by a master basketmaker who must have enjoyed great prestige because of her skill. This basket was probably made as a gift.